WHARNCLIFFE

& OUGHTIBRIDGE PAST

In Pictures

By Andrew Crofts

C000066864

DS Publishing

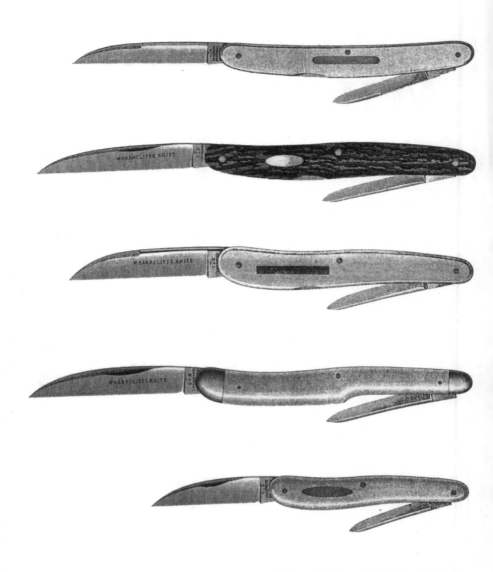

The distinctive serpentine shape of the Wharncliffe Penknife, with its 'Beak' blade, from an 1851 catalogue. Examples shown have stag horn handle, ivory handle and steel handle. The design was said to have been suggested by the Earl of Wharncliffe to Joseph Rodgers, the famous cutler, during an occasion when they were both attending a banquet. At this time Lord Wharncliffe was patron to Joseph's company.

WHARNCLIFFE

& OUGHTIBRIDGE PAST

In Pictures

By Andrew Crofts

© Andrew Crofts 2005

Designed, printed and published by:

DS Publishing
286 South Road
Walkley
Sheffield S6 3TE
Tel: 0114 285 4050
Fax: 0114 285 3050
Email: info@dspad.co.uk
Web: www.dspad.co.uk

ISBN 0-9546769-1-2

Published February 2005

All rights reserved

No part of this publication may be reproduced, stored in a retrieval system or transmitted in any form or by any means, electronic, mechanical, photocopying, recording or otherwise, without prior written permission of the publisher.

All views and comments printed in this book are those of the author and should not be attributed to the publisher.

Acknowledgements

I would like to thank the following people for their generous help in the accumulation of facts and images.

A former work colleague of mine Mr. J. Ambler. Mr. D. Ashton and his mother Mary. Anthea Helliwell. Mr. F. Harvey. The family of the late Mr. James McDonagh. Mrs G. Reid. Mr. R. Deakin. The family of the late Mr. H. Crawshaw. Mrs Marjorie P. Dunn. Mrs Brenda Duffield. The family of the late Mr. E. Morton. The Local History Collection of Sheffield City Library. Grimsby Archives Office. Kelham Island Industrial Museum. Mr. K. Hawley. Mike Parker and Tara Ball at S.V.P. The family of the late Mr. A. Fletcher. Most of all to the memory of my late father, Ben Crofts. and in acknowledgement of his help.

Without their assistance, and that of others I have pestered and 'quizzed' over some years, the original photo collection would have remained a modest stack of mainly 'mystery' pictures.

Foreword

The fact that this project could have started at all owes everything to two photographers who appear to have been busy, a hundred years ago, with roving cameras, in a bid to record something of their village lives at the opening of the twentieth century.

Having been brought up myself in this village, and seeing it escape all but sparse and random mention by different authors of local history at different times, it came as something of a surprise to me to find a record of early photographs here which I might have expected to find in a place of greater size and profile. This being said, the area is still represented by a good few fascinating and largely untapped sources of archive information in Sheffield, which could happily supply a larger work than the one following.

To write about and interpret the pictures of Mr. Robinson and Mr. Fairest, for the benefit of any interested readers seemed to be filling a gap which has long existed in the popular regional histories familiar to many of us up and down the bookshelves. It may also prompt further work on the village by others, in the light of heritage trails soon to come through the area.

Whilst working as an archival photographer, and with an already strong interest in local history, the task of unearthing and matching facts to images seemed like a natural extension to what I was doing during the day anyway, through the last years up to the millennium. It did however take me to library collections in Warwickshire, Grimsby, Hampshire, York, Knottingly and Colindale in London: to name just a few places, in search for the best-sourced explanation of what the two men were illustrating.

More important however than the research into transport history, farming history, manufacturing and social history, where the conversations I had with villagers, some now sadly passed on, who could recall many of the places and characters shown.

The gap of time collapses instantly when a villager, who may only have been a 'schoolkid', apprentice, mill worker, forge worker or farm labourer of the time, is handed one of the prints you have made and can point out facts that only he and his generation of that place could have known. At a time like this there is a need to jot down what is heard as rapidly and accurately as possible, and whilst I didn't always find this easy, is soon became obvious that the best facts were coming by themselves independently of the questions I had prepared.

With these retrieved and "replayed" memories, some frank and illuminating conversations were had about the village of old, and it is to these people that I owe my warmest thanks for keeping the text as well informed as possibly could be.

A. Crofts

CONTENTS

Introduction

Wharncliffe Side, a village which had its name handed down from the making of corn milling stones, ('Quern-cliff'), has occupied a pleasant valley in several forms, since the Romano-Britons lived there. It has a wooded crag to its east and sloping meadow fields, cut by two winding brooks to the north and west. The river Don crosses the floor of the valley going south towards the city, and is added to at two different points by the brooks. In days gone by visitors have described the valley as two landscapes in one; wild, forested and rocky on one side, lush green pasture with the sound of running waters on the other.

The poet John Taylor in the 1630s, thought enough about the picturesque beauty of Wharncliffe to write about it in length, as did John Holland later in the 1830s; and Walter Scott, after his 1819 stay at the high lodge on top of the crag, had been moved to write the opening lines of his epic story 'Ivanhoe'. The crag itself was celebrated in ballad and legend by way of a fierce dragon and a brave knight, the 'Dragon of Wantly' and his adversary 'More of More Hall'. This was a local folklore story noted for its strong medieval flavour, of chivalric bravery and a knight's code. Not surprisingly it inspired Victorian writers and painters alike, particularly the followers of the Pre-Raphaelite movement.

In the middle of the nineteenth century, with the spread of knowledge on the new science of photography, a Sheffield optician Theopolis Smith concentrated his attention on this area to produce a series of photographs which were thought to be the earliest taken in Sheffield. These were made using the wet collodion process that he had mastered, and they showed various features of the crag, ones associated with the dragon myth, the 'Dragon's Cave' and the 'Dragon's Well'.

By 1899 the interest and following enjoyed by photography was well represented in Sheffield where the city's photographic society had sixty two members. Photographic postcards were particularly popular in the period 1900 to 1910; as a message and a 'view' could be sent for just one half-penny postage. Names like Robert Sneath and Sam Morgan were known for the prolific production of Sheffield views for postcards at this time. The breadth of subjects being sought by the professionals began to be echoed in the work of a few gifted amateurs.

Around this time, two local photographers, Luther Fairest and Herbert Robinson took, what for a small area was a good sized collection of photographs of local interest, both in the valley and at the neighbouring village of Oughtibridge. Although they were both amateurs, Herbert's camera produced 4¾" X 6½" glass plates known as the 'Half-Plate' size, which photographers recognise as serious large-format work. Luther was known to produce pictures for a local newspaper the Penistone, Stocksbridge & Hoyland Express. Both had other jobs, at a time when typically a villager's occupation could blur into several incarnations at the same time, in order to keep the wolf from the door. One of the lasting and re-occurring memories of Herbert seems to be that anyone could take a pair of boot tops to him, that is worn out boot with the soles all but gone, and from these he would make a fine pair of clogs, with many years use ahead of them. He would do this moreover for much less than the cost of new boots. He doesn't appear to have had a studio, such as they were then, but preferred to take his plate camera out and about. He lived in an ivy-fronted house on School Lane, Wharncliffe Side; one of a row now demolished. A recent chance-find of some of his pictures has revealed features of landscape, people and buildings of great local historical interest.

The condition of these glass plates, when found, along with Herbert's technical skill all those years ago, has made sure of a high quality of image by and large. Whilst I was printing the negatives, the faces and figures which emerged looked as if they had been captured the previous week rather than some ninety five years ago. The only thing which seemed to give them away, an un-fakable feature, were their eyes. Here to my mind is the evidence of a much harder era, wherein people needed to be physically tougher to a certain extent, more self-reliant and perhaps more wary. The welfare state, many of the notions of 'safety at work' and a good few individual rights were still nearly half a century away. However, this being the case, they obviously made the most of what they had, because a warm community spirit coupled with dignity shows through too, both in the group pictures and those of individuals.

In this book I have set out ten themed chapters, with Mr. Robinson's pictures as the main illustrators of each topic, to say something about village life in general. Other pictures, some being Mr. Fairest's have been used where available, to give extra useful information, and there are some present day images included for comparisons.

I hope that as you browse through you will feel the subject opening out to you in a way which makes you able to add your own reminiscences, from re-lighted memories; then to return to the book again and again, the way good evocative reference material always invites us to.

Approaching the Village

Approaching the village from the south, in the 1900s, presented this view; a view of a mill! To this day the view still shows many of the same features, although the old square chimney has now gone, demolished in the mid 1970's. We are looking down from a high cliff edge called Crag View, chosen I think for the

good view of the works it gave. The main turnpike road passes very close to this paper mill, and goes on through to the village beyond. Some details of the village can be seen in the distance. The river Don at the right also follows roughly this north/south line, as does the railway line in the woods, even further right, but off the picture.

To come down to the road level and move closer to the mill shows how, early in the century there were buildings on either side of the road; the main mill ones on the right, and some store sheds on the left. A newspaper article in the Sheffield Independant, dated August 14th, 1886 describes these sheds as being piled to the roof with bales of Esparto grass and cotton rags, then used together to manufacture the newsprint paper used by that very same publication. This was a stouter and more durable newsprint than the present day ones in use, with less tendancy to fading and darkening, and rarely if ever became brittle. It made good sense to keep the raw materials just outside the mill like this, especially ones as flammable as the grasses, until just before they were to be used.

Further still and we are entering the village. The Wharncliffe Arms pub stands solidly on the right, then with a flagpole. After a stretch of roadside housing, in the distance is the old school, with its original bell tower. The turnoff to the left before that is Green Lane, which then had a sign on the turning advertising 'Glen

Howe Tower', a park attraction to be found a short walk to the west.

If you were to walk up close to the school, and then look back, this is the view you would have seen. The mill never seems to dominate the village because it lies on lower ground, so there is a kind of rural tranquility, even close to industry. The sign on the left showing 'Strouts' ales belonged to a little pub tucked away in the bend of the road, called the 'Travellers Inn'. This then was the village, at its most widely used point of entry. Many of the details which follow will keep referring back to this relatively small area.

Local Services

The year of 1900, the bright opening year of the new century started out with Sheffield suffering the slight inconvenience of having to do without street lighting for one hour every night. This happened on January 5th when it was decided that, because of a coal famine, the supply of town gas for street lighting would have to be cut to conserve stocks. The cuts went on through most of the winter.

The people of Wharncliffe Side would have found this quite amusing, as their streets were in darkness all night and every night, they always had been. The gas supply at this time, from the 'Sheffield Gas Light Company' came up as far as Oughtibridge, and included the paper mill. From this there would have been a low-level glow of illumination from the main road at night. Apart from that however, oil lamps provided the sole means of lighting for the Wharncliffe villager. It was a common sight to see white dots of light tracing the hillsides and lanes at finish if work in winter. A trek home from one of the small workshops, or the paper mill could take quite a while in those days. Gas light did finally come, in around 1910, and it was much welcomed.

As illustrations of local services I have found, in picture form, both local post offices, the village policeman's house, and some services run for profit:- milk delivery and the 'Entire Horse'.

In the 1880s, if you wanted to make a telephone call, it seems you would have to go to the house of a Mr. Woodcock, whole premises was listed officially as 'John Henry Woodcock; Baker Confectioner and National Telephone Call Office'. This place, in Oughtibridge, became the manual switchboard building. The yard outside became known as Telephone Yard on Orchard Street. There were very few telephones then in Wharncliffe Side, and the few there were would not have been for general public use. An instance of emergency would have been the only time when an ordinary villager made use of a telephone installed at any of the bigger houses, and even then the call would have been made on his or her behalf by the householders. Illnesses and accidents would have accounted for most of these. The only really great emergency of this period was the paper mill fire of 1899. Then a telephone was used to call up the fire brigade. Spring Grove Paper Mill itself carried the telephone number 1. The mill owner's house Spring Grove House carried the number of 2. and the Wharncliffe Arms pub carried the number 3.

We see a Spring morning not long after the turn of the century; and something which was a reoccurring sight in the village, Walter Holmes and the 'Entire Horse'. This horse belonged to a local stud owner, Mr W. Green, but Walter was the man given the job to lead it around the various farms of the locality to sire new working animals; thus keeping the wheels of the rural workaday world turning. It was essentially a commercial venture, run by 'Billy' Green as he was known, but it was always recognised too as a valuable service for the farming community.

12

The year was 1907, the height of the horse drawn age. It was a well known fact at the time that if a farm needed new working horses, then to go out and find them, choose the best ones at sales, and then bring them home, could mean a hefty bill in transport cost, lost work time, auctioneers purchase premium etc. Bidding prices too could be subject to an unexpected rise, which could be unwelcome news to

farmers on low budgets. If a modest stud fee could compete with this, then the advantage of siring new foals amongst the mares of your own existing teams could soon become obvious.

Outside the Wharncliffe Arms pub, then sporting the telephone number of '3' on the best room, Walter and friend are getting ready to set off at around nine in the morning for a trek which will take them around all the farms at which they have an appointment this day. Some may have been called at speculatively. The route was roughly circular, calling at some fairly isolated places, and finishing up back at this pub or the one of the horse's owner. Mr. Green ran a pub himself, and had arrangements with other ones so that Walter could call there for stabling and feeding if needed.

Some twelve or thirteen weeks were used as the season for this trekking, and many miles would be covered. Owners would typically have a target of 100 mares to be served. The stud card shown here shows the terms and conditions of business typically in use during the first half of the 20th century, along with a tariff. On our friend's back can be seen a pack, held on by a wide strap known as a 'Roller'. The pack contains the horse's cleaning and conditioning tools, a brush and 'Curry Comb', some hoof oil, and a lightweight waterproof cloth to cover his back in rainy weather. At times (though not here) there may have been a small measure of maize or oats as a snack, supplementing his main feeding times (hay was freely available at most pubs). Also carried in the bundle would be a nosebag, and very probably a set of 'Hobbling Cords'. This

TERMS FOR ALL STALLIONS:

£4 FOR EACH MARE

Due July 15th. All Fees that have to be collected after this date will be charged 10/- extra.

Groom's Fee, 5s. (to be paid at time of service).

Barren Mares from 1945, £2.

Stud Groom : Richard Singleton.

CONDITIONS.

All Mares at Owner's risk.

The Owner accepts no responsibility whatsoever for accidents arising through Mares being tried or served, or through any other cause, but every reasonable care will be taken.

No Mare served twice within the space of eleven days, the Groom in charge to decide whether Mares are fit for service.

All Mares tried to be paid for.

Every possible care will be taken, but none of the parties concerned shall be liable for any damages through mishap to the Stallions, Grooms, Mares or Attendants during trial or service.

The Owner reserves the right to substitute one horse for another or alter the routes should the necessity arise.

Further information from Groom in charge, or Owner, R. SUTTON, Moor House, Longton.

Tel. : Longton 101.

was simply a loosely-worn cord restraint to be placed on mares seen to be nervous, thus preventing them from kicking out at him at a crucial moment. All these were folded up with great neatness and compactness. It wasn't unknown for some stallions to be trimmed up with ribbons and plumes in order to impress those farmers who were seen as important potential customers. Walter's charge was known to be from excellent stock, and this was always appreciated. It was generally known when the travels were going to start, and where from, as a few lines of information usually made an appearance in the farming notes of the local newspaper. The 9 am start was good practise too, as it gave time for farmers who were not on or near the route to bring in their on-heat mares and 'intercept' Walter as he was getting ready to go. They sometimes did this believing that the first service of the day was going to be the best.

The post office was the next building up from the Wharncliffe Arms, going north. It appears to have been an Alladin's cave of items, indeed the shop's sign tells us that the proprieter, Mr. Albert Brooke, was a florist, fruiterer and greengrocer. The window of this post office was on the gable end of a row of dwellings known as 'Post Office Row'. I have been told that when customers entered here at the left, Mr. Brooke would emerge from a trap door in the floor to serve them. Having lived in apartments behind and under this room for some years, he preferred the 'Will Mossop' method of moving between house and shop. To anyone new to the village I can imagine this being something of a shock, particularly if you were standing close to, or on the trap at the time! The box in which the shutters were kept took its place to the right of the window, and the posting slit for letters can be seen between the shutter box and the window.

14

Although this was a post office, it could not receive telegraph messages. The nearest telegraph office was Oughtibridge. Nor could it cash postal orders, only issue them. The goods on display include biscuits and sweets in jars, two board games, matches, postcards and comics, safety pins, pocket knives, heel pads, boxes of chocolate and toffee, fruit, brawn, fish, eggs, crockery and shoe polish. Before this post office opened, the postal service in Wharncliffe Side consisted simply of a wall box, which had a collection at 8.00 a.m. and 7.50 p.m. weekdays only. Clearly this shop had to supply many of the needs of the villagers, and it didn't forget the youngsters!

The three comics on display are 'Butterfly', 'Chips' and 'Funny Cuts'; from the golden age of Edwardian comics. They are dated the 15th, 16th and 19th of November 1907.

The half-penny comic 'Chips' was owned by the press baron Alfred Harmsworth (later to become known as Lord Northcliffe). In 1904 Harmsworth struck a deal with Joseph Dixon the papermaker, which amounted to an order for 200 tons of newsprint paper per week over five years. Harmsworth's chain-ownership of newspapers and publications was hungry for supplies of paper. The deal was worth three-quarters of a million pounds; and it was a source of great pride to the mill workers and Mr. Dixon that it was the quality of the paper and its finish that had been the deciding factor in the deal. It may be then, that the comics we are looking at in this picture were produced on Dixon paper.

Post Office Row was, as can be seen, quite a long building, with several houses in addition to the post office in it, stretching away from the road. It was eventually demolished and replaced by a two-storey brick dwelling with a shop front, which survives today as a house. Mr. Brooke, however, retained some of the footing of the old building where it occupied the bottom of his garden, and put a greenhouse on it.

The garden wall, with its big cornerstone in the foreground, is seemingly the only feature still surviving today from this 1907 picture. At the base of the stone is carved the date of 1891, and the initials 'CB'. This may be referring to another of the Brooke family, perhaps Albert's father.

15

'CHIPS,' ½D.

£5 A WEEK
FOR FOLLOWERS
OF FOOTBALL!

If you take any interest in football,
see the Editor's grand offer inside.
£5 for somebody every week. An
absolutely equal chance for every-
body. One reader, one attempt.

'THE MOTOR MAN,' CHIPS' GRAND NEW STORY, STARTS TO-DAY.

ILLUSTRATED CHIPS

1D ½

No. 898. (NEW SERIES.) [ENTERED AT STATIONERS' HALL.] PRICE ONE HALFPENNY. [TRANSMISSION ABROAD AT BOOK RATES.] NOVEMBER 16, 1907.

WEARY WILLIE AND TIRED TIM VISIT "CHIPS" OFFICE—AND FEEL SORRY.

1. Willie and Tim had a silly joke played on them the other dewy morn. The postman brought a nice fat, heavy parcel, and both thought it might be a valuable present from Corney Chips. But, alas! it turned out to be a very cheap sort of brick.

2. Of course, it was a terrible blow to our pair; but, as Tim remarked, it might have been worse—Corney might have paid someone to throw it at them. So they crept towards Chips' Office. But, stay! it looks as if they were expected slightly, doesn't it?

3. Yes; old Corney Chips, Bottles the office boy, and the lady typist were all on the look-out, but managed to bob out of sight as our pair came round the bend. "This is a bit of all-right, sonny," chirped Tim when they discovered the pulleys round at the back of the premises.

4. Having gained an entry to the building, the first person they met was Bottles. "Menial," said Willie severely, "leave off tearing your face and conduct us to your master!"

5. A little later the pair leaped forward with a wild, glad cry. "'Ere he is!" shouted Tim, "playing at being a bunch of grass. Kumoutovit!"

6. More disappointment! It wasn't Corney at all, but just the office mop, with a little bay rum sprayed over it to put our pair off the scent. Then the fighting editor strolled in—

7. And, picking the trouble merchants up by the scruff of their waistcoats, deliberately threw them out of a window into the murky Thames.

8. Then they had a ride in a dredger, and the gent who was minding it had best part of a fit when he saw what he had keeched up in the course of business. 16-11-7

9. Finally, the pair were arrested. We don't know on what charge; in fact, the policeman doesn't know himself yet, but he's sure to think up something before he gets to the station.

The front page characters of Chips, were two likeable tramps 'Tired Tim and Weary Willie'. They had appeared at the startup of the comic in 1896, and continued on for the best part of sixty years.

A one-horse cart was the means by which the milk was delivered in 1906, which was when this picture was taken. William Grayson, seen here with measuring cans in hand, was the milkman in days long before bottled deliveries operated, even in city suburbs. Behind him to the right is the row of cottages which was known as 'Saw Pit Row'. These have since been demolished; but the ones directly beside him to the left have in recent years been restored and modernised. It was a common sight to see the younger members of families being sent to William with a jug, straight from the kitchen. Into this would be poured a set measure of the untreated full-cream milk, to be carefully carried back for the day's requirements.

Leisure

Although in statistical terms the pub years of highest national popularity had passed, being 1850-1877, the public house remained an important social and recreational focus for the working classes. There were 100,000 of them in England and Wales at the time Herbert was taking his pictures of Wharncliffe Side. The village boasted three pubs:- the 'Wharncliffe Arms', the 'Traveller's Inn' and the 'Blue Ball Inn'. (formerly the 'Blue Dumpling'). These were all roadside buildings, ranged along the main road through the settlement.

Sporting pastimes followed on from the growing interest in the Football League, formed in 1888, and the County Cricket Championship in 1873. In little villages like this amateurs wanted to emulate the heroic teams on the 'national stage', so they would get together to do so whenever they could. The mill owner's house had its own tennis court, but this could hardly have been said to be for village use. A nearby park in Howe Wood gave a chance to play some sports; though in a hilly village like this there was rarely a chance to use an absolutely level surface.

The Wharncliffe Arms was one of the better class of pubs, it having 'Provision for Cyclists' and 'Good Stabling' ostensibly for the use of the customers, as this picture shows. The landlord at the time was Mr. John William Bisby, who was a relative newcomer, having just taken over from Mr. Frank Handley at the turn of the century.

The beer of this pub in those days came from A.H. Smith's 'Don Brewery' on Penistone Road, a brewery which, during its lifetime owned 108 pubs and supplied a range of beers which, these days would spoil us for choice. One of their own advertisements of the time shows that they were brewers of mild and strong ales, bitter beer, light bitter beer, and also stout.

As well as being landlord of this pub Mr. Bisby was a dealer in hay. It was, I am told possible to walk through to the back of the building, to where the hay was kept, by going into the stable on the right and through a door at the back of the horse stall. There was a further door at the north-east corner of the building which shows signs of having been blocked up for many years now.

One of A.H. Smith's better known beers was 'Old Tom' or 'XXXXX' beer, a dark, rich brew which was a particular favourite amongst Sheffield grinders, as it soothed dust-choked throats. Later in time, after 1916 when the brewery had been taken over by Tennant Brothers, a dark mild beer became available called 'Wharncliffe Ale'.

ESTABLISHED 1832.

Telegraphic Address:
"DON BREWERY, SHEFFIELD."

Telephone No. 319.

A. H. SMITH & CO. Lᴛᴅ.,

DON BREWERY,

PENISTONE ROAD,

SHEFFIELD,

BREWERS OF

MILD ᴀɴᴅ STRONG ALES,

BITTER BEER AND STOUT,

LIGHT BITTER BEER FOR FAMILY USE

At 1/- per gallon, in 9, 12 and 18 gall. Casks.

BOTTLERS OF ALE AND STOUT.

WINE, SPIRIT AND CIGAR

MERCHANTS.

SOLE PROPRIETORS OF THE FAMOUS

"GLEN SHEE" SPECIAL SCOTCH WHISKY.
AND THE
"SHAN" SPECIAL IRISH WHISKY.

The Traveller's Inn, pictured in 1908, was just a few yards away from the Wharncliffe Arms, northwards along the main road, still in the older part of the village. The road here begins an uphill curve, so the traveller may well have been tempted to stop and take fortification before continuing, as the name suggests. The landlord at this time was William Clarke Fairweather, and the beer was 'Strouts Ales', made at the Burton Road brewery at Neepsend. This was another business which was taken over by Edward and Robert Tennant during the First World War.

In another view of the Wharncliffe Arms from the south we can get a wider impression of its surroundings. To the right of it, on the branch-off from the main road is the house which was known as Dumpling Hall, built in the early part of the nineteenth century, and home at this time of the mill owner's chauffeur Mr. Blowers.

Beyond the pub is the building which became Post Office Row. The fact that the large wooden window surround with shutter box has not yet been built, tells us that this picture was taken before 1907. The sign saying 'Don Brewery Entire' refers to a kind of ale which was a blend of two medium priced brown ales, along with a more expensive light ale; a mix sometimes called the 'Three Threads'. This had been available in public houses as far back as the eighteenth century, but initially had had to be blended by the landlord himself. Eventually the breweries sold it ready mixed, so it became yet another beer available from A.H. Smith's Don Brewery; 'Entire Ale'.

The Blue Ball Inn seen here getting a clean and scrub in its smart marble doorway was the third roadside pub, standing to this day at the northern end of the village, near where the main road leaves the valley. Its name originally was the 'Blue Dumpling', so named after a local fondness for making dumplings out of bilberries, a very tasty and economical dessert. For many years however, the inn's sign was accompanied by a hanging ball, as indeed the photograph shows, and eventually the term 'Blue Ball' stuck, the other dying away.

At the time this picture was taken, around 1907, the Blue Ball was a farm as well as a public house, and the publican Frederick Siddons was officially listed as a 'Farmer and

Victualler' as indeed was the publican before him. The fact that the pub worked as a farm is apparent in the south door, the one nearest to us in the picture. Today this door is completely blocked up, but when Mr. Siddons was there it opened in two parts like a stable door.

Sometimes the Blue Ball was the site of livestock sales. Animals would be brought down from the hill farms and auctioned. The buyers could be other farmers, or perhaps local butchers like Mr. J. Hayward of Oughtibridge. Drovers were then often hired on the spot to move the animals along the main road to their new destinations. This was a time when, by law, livestock animals took precedence over wheeled transport in the use of the highways. The driver of a cart, cab, omnibus, steam vehicle or motor car could be in serious trouble if he failed to give way to, or otherwise made things difficult for a drover and his animals.

When these auctions were going on, some deals were invariably struck up over a glass of ale; so you could say that the activities of work and leisure came together here. Even for those who were not actually taking part in the sales, the sight of a prize bull being led up and down outside the pub, or a group of best milking cows being penned in the yard for the perusal of buyers, must inevitably have drawn a fair amount of interest and attention.

This view of the White Hart in Oughtibridge, taken in 1905 by Luther Fairest shows again how public houses were the resting stops of the horse-drawn age. The stable block on the right shows two arched doorways, one of which is blocked up, the other

21

clearly in use as a stable door, with ventilating slats in the top. Above that is a round hatch for storage of hay in the loft, as seen on so many farms of the district. Coumes Brook runs beneath this building, in a fast underground dash, its last few yards before reaching the Don.

Another leisure activity popular at this time was the mass excursion. On an evidently clear morning, August 8th 1908, the staff of Spring Grove Paper Mill went on a works outing to London.

Although the message on the picture was rather untidily done, we have to remember that photographers then literally painted written details on to the emulsion side of a negative to make them appear on finished prints. This meant that they had to write everything in reverse, which isn't easy. Some photographers were better at it than others. The information is the important thing which has come down to us. The picture shows around sixty people waiting on the platform of Oughtibridge Station, which at this time was owned by the Great Central Railway Company.

The trip was for the purpose of visiting the Franco-British Exhibition of 1908, a scientific and cultural exhibition, at which it was possible to see a great many of the new advances that had been made in industry. Companies from both sides of the channel proudly displayed their machinery and products on the huge exhibition site near the centre of

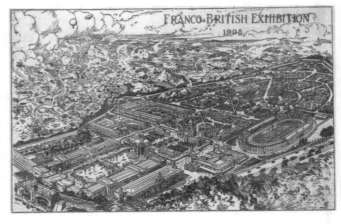

London, and an interested public came from far and wide to see.

The popularity of such exhibitions was high, following on from the Great Exhibition of 1851, and rather than passing away like a fad it mingled with the enthusiasm for the 'Entente Cordialle' celebrations and events that were taking place at this time. Britain's new relationship with France stood to gain by this coming together of exhibitors, especially when each government considered the trade and export orders which could follow.

There were displays of art and cuisine, printing, horticulture, heavy and light engineering, scientific instruments, pharmaceuticals ...the list was almost endless. Brightly coloured cafes and restaurants provided refreshments in either the English or French style, and there were frequent musical performances to listen to if so desired.

A French company did, in fact have a display comprising papermaking technique and machinery, and it could have been that Joseph Dixon wanted to see this, as he was always a man to study the state of play in his own industry, both as it stood in Britain and abroad. It seems that on this occasion he wanted the workforce to have a chance to see it too. He financed the trip, paying everyone's fare, and granting each employee two shillings for refreshments.

The train which the day trippers were waiting for was a local stopping train, which would have come from Penistone. At this time it was possible to catch a train coming through from Penistone at 8 o'clock in the morning, and then to change in Sheffield for the 8.50 morning express to London. In the event though, the local train was late in arriving at Oughtibridge, and so it was noon before Sheffield was left behind. The party arrived in London at 3.40.

At the nearest end, we can see a line-up of flat-capped, but smartly turned-out men waiting near one of the platform gas lamps. The hampers on the barrow in the background could well have contained packed lunches to be eaten on the way, as this was quite a long journey. It is safe to assume that the London train would have had a restaurant car, but the prices would have been quite out of the range of the pockets of these people. Some advertising of the time can be seen on the side of one of the boxes, 'Cakeoma'; an early brand of self-raising flour, famed for 'The Lightest of Cakes'.

23

The gas lamp bears the name of the station, and this, along with a large sign on the down platform opposite always carried the spelling of Oughtibridge with a 'Y', and split into two words. This was always known as the 'railway spelling' of the name, and had been so since the opening of the station in 1845.

Upon entering the exhibition this grand pavilion called Congress Hall was the first sight to welcome visitors. A more general view of the exhibition can be seen at the bottom of the picture. The railway company was keen to promote its arrangements for getting to the showground, as can be seen from the map of Undergound stops. One of the earliest 'Tube' lines to be built; this line, the Central London Railway (now the Central Line) proudly announced that it could carry visitors from their arrival points right in to Exhibition Station; specially built for the purpose. This station is now called White City. A loop was put in at Wood Lane to enable trains to run more or less continuously. This poster was one of several produced for CLR in August 1908 in relation to the show, which had started in the spring.

Exhibitor's stands inevitably became company advertisements, as can be seen in this one for Martell the French Brandy producers. Others attending were Moet & Chandon's, Burgoyne's Wine Pavilion, Schweppes, Farrar's Toffee House from Harrogate, the Bovril Pavilion, Coalite, Perrier Table Water Co., Mc Vitie & Price, the list went on. There were boating lakes with islands on them, sporting cascades of water which were illuminated at night, an Olympic standard stadium where the 1908 Olympics were being held at the very same time. Model cities of the world and fairground rides like the 'Flipflap' captured people's attention, and a moving picture palace showed the latest examples of the exciting new invention, 'Cinematographic Films'. Other attractions included a working bakery, a confectionery plant, a model working dairy, a mineral water factory and a special glass making plant.

EXPOSITION FRANCO-BRITANNIQUE

PAVILLON · J & F. MARTELL · COGNAC

Even by today's standards this would have been an entertaining day out, and I have often wondered what it would have been like to have been with the villagers on that day. Though of modest incomes, they were nonetheless shown the very best that the Edwardian age then had to offer.

Cricket was often played in the village at this time, the best place being the flattest and lowest part of the valley, the fields between Long Wood and the river.

Here we see the Wharncliffe Side cricket team of 1908 in West Holme Field, one of the fields of Dyson Holmes on the floor of the valley. To the left is the pavilion hut, built to hold a changing room and to keep scores on a large panel at the back. Rising up behind the group is Wharncliffe Wood, showing only thin tree cover at this period because of frequent clearing which was done in the nineteenth century.

What I like about this picture, looking more closely, is the classic Edwardian sportsmanlike appearance of some of the players; in cricket whites and caps, with at least one handlebar moustache visible - appearances cultivated in the spirit of the game as it was then. Even the spectators are sporting straw boaters, bowlers, smart jackets and cravats. Lord Hawke, the captain of Yorkshire at this time would have approved, not least because of the sense of occasion it gave to the game.

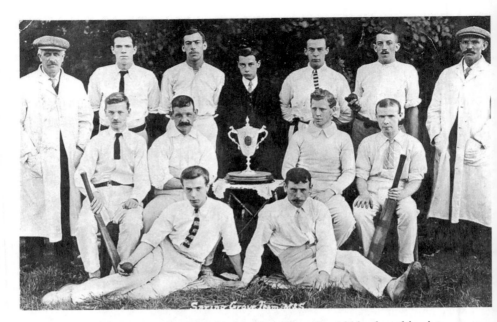

Later on, cricket became more organised in the village. By 1913 when this picture was taken, the paper mill had its own team. In that particularly successful year they won the Wadsley Cup, visible in the centre of the group. This was the last year of peace before the Great War; and most of the men seen in this picture were called up to fight in France from September of the following year.

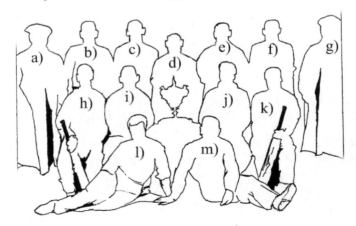

a) A. Crawshaw b) G. Holmes c) J. Brooke d) A. Marshall e) S. Cardwell f) H. Rhodes g) R. Bullock h) W. Wood i) H. Earnshaw j) G. Wood k) Mr. Ibbotson? l) W. Cardwell m) J. Paget.

This village football side of eleven lads in mid-teens was photographed in 1907, and is fairly typical of many such amateur teams that were being formed in the first decade of the twentieth century. Although none of their names are known, or the exact whereabouts of the pitch they are playing on on this occasion, I have been told that they traditionally played on the land just behind the Blue Ball Inn. That area then consisted of fairly broad open fields. A later picture, of the 1920s, shows the village eleven lined up within the cobbled yard of the Blue Ball.

The standards of skill and organisation in these amateur clubs were heavily influenced by the professional ones they were trying to emulate, and had grown impressively in the last twenty years of the nineteenth century. The ball we see is a leather 'case' version, and would have had an inner 'bladder' of rubber, put in through a gap which could be laced up after it was inflated. In wet conditions this ball would have become quite heavy, requiring more and more powerful kicks to move it. A coating of dubbin applied before the game could help to stave off this problem, but it was always a delicate balancing act between the 'greasy, slippery ball' and the 'heavy sodden ball'. It must have taken a degree of endurance to play in hobnailedl football boots and shin-length trousars held up by snake belts!

Workplaces

The work ethic of the Wharncliffe Side area was strong, and, like many small villages of the West Riding at that time, the type of work which supported people included farming, the work of the small forge, and that of the small cutlery finishing shops. In addition to this a number of stone quarries were worked in the area, especially on the rim of the valley. The author of 'The Story of Wortley Ironworks', Mr. C. Reginald Andrews, recalled that the age-old craft of the charcoal burner was still visible in Wharncliffe Wood when he passed through on a train just before 1900. It must be said that at that time the use of charcoal as a fuel for ironworking had all but disappeared in favour of coke, but hung on in the form of the 'blister' steel process. The small 'Dyson Holmes Tilt', a works near the river was engaged in the making of 'shear' steel around this period. Further downstream from that was a small cornmill. Both these concerns used water power to drive their machinery.

Men and women of Wharncliffe Side did file cutting by hand in their own domestic environment, and cutlery finishing was practised also on a family basis, often by people who additionally farmed the land. It was not unusual to see a shed or workshop of ramshackle appearance either adjoining someone's dwelling, or in the garden. There are records too of a smithy and 'saw-pit' located at the northern end of the village. These were the small rural businesses which were common in many Yorkshire villages at the time.

Wharncliffe Side however had something extra to this. A medium sized factory stood at the southern entrance to the valley, and it was called 'Spring Grove Mill'.

This was a business started up by a Mr. William Jenkinson in 1834 for the production of gun wadding and paper. It actually carried an Oughtibridge postal address, and still does to this day; but to the traveller reaching it along the main road it appears to stand about a mile from Oughtibridge proper, and yet almost inamongst the houses of Wharncliffe. The owner was not too successful in this business, and soon sold the

Peter Dixon 1817-1882

Peter Dixon 1817-1882

mill to Mollet, Hough and Brassington. It wasn't so very long however before it was passed on yet again, this time being sold to the Marsh Brothers of Pond Hill, Sheffield. After this rapid and not-too-happy transfer of ownership through the hands of three operators, none of them very successful, a man came along who would become the most well known and liked mill owner of the area; Peter Dixon Esq. Dixon belonged to a family from Morley, West Yorkshire and already had several paper business connections in Scotland. He purchased the mill from the Marsh brothers in 1871 for the sum of £8,500, and with his son Joseph in joint control, moved the firm on to a much greater degree of success than any of the predecessors had managed.

Peter only lived to see the first part of this success, as he died early in the new year of 1882. Joseph however, continued after him with the kind of growing prosperity which comes from knowledge of the product and good business sense.

Here we see Spring Grove Mill in the late 1890s, featured in a document printed when it had just quadrupled its production of paper. When Mr. Dixon purchased the business it was turning out 10 tons of paper per week. By the time this photograph was taken it was producing just in excess of 40 tons per week, and the figure continued to rise through the turn of the century. All the output had a ready and eager market waiting for it. The picture shows the mill as it could be seen from a high point to the south, called Crag

Spring Grove Paper Mill,

Mill Number 969.   OUGHTY BRIDGE.   ESTABLISHED 1871.

Near SHEFFIELD.

View. Thick woods now obscure this view; but in Mr. Robinson's time it was the best place to view the layout of the factory in its entirety. The 'established' date of 1871 seen on the right refers to when the Dixons acquired the works rather than when it was built.

Peter Dixon & Son LIMITED.
PAPERMAKERS

HEAD OFFICE,
SPRING GROVE PAPER MILLS,
OUGHTIBRIDGE, NR SHEFFIELD.

In August of 1888 a legal agreement was drawn up between Joseph Dixon and the railway company who owned the Sheffield to Manchester line, which passes through Wharncliffe Woods (the area to the right of the picture). This was to construct a single, private branch line, starting at Oughtibridge station. The line would make its way in a 2 mile gradual curve downhill through the wood, towards the mill. Once it reached the river it would traverse a railway bridge (the one in the picture) which was to be specially constructed for the purpose, and then continue into the heart of the works. The work of laying down this private siding, cutting a way through the woods, and building the bridge was to be carried out by the Manchester,

29

Sheffield and Lincolnshire Railway Company, at a cost of £750. The Dixons duly paid this sum to the company and the work was begun in the same year. Once linked by points to the main line, this siding, one of several serving firms near the station, made the deliveries of fuel, coal from the Yorkshire and Nottinghamshire coalfields much more reliable than with the road shipments which had to be used before. Raw materials of pulp, clay and chemicals were also brought in by rail. However, road transport continued to be used. The finished product, newsprint paper, was shipped out by both rail and road at this time, soon to be ably assisted by a Coulthard steam lorry, acquired during the first decade of the 20th century.

Here was the area where all the mill's road traffic came and went, then and now. This picture is another from the late 1890s, and it shows a delivery of hay, used for stabling the mill's draught horses, being taken in at one of the loft doors which opened to the road. Most of the left-hand buildings seen here are today used by the engineering section of the firm, and a large road entrance is now situated at the left foreground. On the right hand side of the road can be seen the stacked bales of raw materials; rags and Esparto grass, used in

papermaking. The old original square-built chimney with its fluted top rose to a height of 75 ft.

These boilermen are working with two large Lancashire boilers, which, at Spring Grove Mill were partly open to the air, in an arrangement which appears to have favoured the bringing in of the fuel. The coal could come down to the boiler fronts in railway trucks which had hinged bottoms, thus allowing the men to release each load at the closest point for shovelling.

The boilers have two stoking hatches each, and they were made by a firm called James Howden & Co. There are in fact three boilers in the picture. The third one, barely visible amongst the piping stands at the back. The general practise was to run two boilers and keep one at rest for cleaning and routine maintenance. Howden was a Glasgow firm which had, through the 19th century, earned itself a name for success in heavy engineering and steam power. As well as the steam boilers there were at least two stationary steam engines in the mill, one of which was a Howden engine. The idea was that the steam produced by the boilers would be piped to the engines at their various locations, at anything up to 160 p.s.i.. They, when set in motion would drive first a fly-wheel, then via belts and shafts, all the factory machinery. This system of drive using wheels, belts and shafts was known as 'line-shafting'. It ran from room to room, workshop to workshop, usually at ceiling height, and was the way all production lines of this age were driven, before the time of a national electrical grid. The loud slapping of belts, the rumbling of wheels and hiss of steam was a sound well known to mill workers of the 1900s, and the whole setup needed the vigilant attention of a 'Millwright' to keep it running. Spring Grove Mill did, however, use some electricity at this time, but not a great deal of power was consumed. Such that was came from the mill's own generator which was turned by water.

The men's job was to keep the boilers fuelled from the trucks, and to regulate the steam pressure. The man to the right of the picture was Bernard (Spriggy) Ellison. Normally the men would be on an eight hour, three shift system, and the two boilers in use would be running round the clock. It was hard work. In 1902, one ton of saleable paper was produced for every two tons of coal burned for steam power here. By 1912 the consumption was down to thirteen and a half hundredweight for the same production. In winter sometimes, a canvas cover would be hung over this frontal area to keep in as much heat as possible. The buildup of sulphurous fumes under this cover did itself constitute quite a health hazard. The handles on the boiler fronts marked Open and Shut were 'dampers', for regulating the flow of air. The open position was for 'firing-up' the boiler to its maximum operating temperature when a lot of steam was required. The shut position would level-off the heat, or let it die down gradually in preparation for 'shut-down' times, when cleaning and maintenance would be done. Stoking had to be done quickly and with a good aim, throwing the coal to the furthest end of the grate as possible, through the narrow hatch, without spilling any. The men would close the damper, to prevent flames from spraying out, open the hatch, then between them shovel the coal with the strongest throwing action they could manage, doing it rhythmically and in turn, until they had completed that particular 'charge'. The hatch would then be shut and the damper opened up again.

After a boiler had been shut down it could take days for it to cool down sufficiently to allow for cleaning and sweeping out the old ash. The water bearing part of the boiler would need attention also; to clear it of the crusty scale that would have gathered there. This would entail having to physically climb inside the water chamber, after it had been drained, and scrape away at the scale until it was clear. This was known as the 'Fluer's' job; not very envied, as there was often still some residual heat in the water chamber, making this not a comfortable task. During alterations to one of the flues, a

Mr. M. Wordsworth was fatally injured in the year this picture was taken, 1907. He apparently suffered a fractured skull. This ended a remarkable 40-year record of fatality-free working at the paper mill. You have to go back to 1870, the year before the Dixon's takeover to find any others.

When the coal trucks came down to the boilers, the locomotive bringing them could not come all the way down the siding, (shunting time was expensive). Until the mill got a shunting engine of its own, much of the distance was dealt with using draught horses, kept at the mill for the purpose. Raw materials and chemicals were brought in this way too. Here we can see a horse-drawn rail truck just  crossing the railway bridge, shortly before the turn of the century. We can see also some of the effects of one of the fires of the 1890s. Charred woodwork on the left of the picture, and bent steel girders amongst the rubble on the right bear witness to the ferocity of one of the fires. Miraculously the bridge seems unaffected, and the river itself has acted as a natural barrier, protecting the buildings on the East side. Those were built in the mid-1890s, and parts of them, the lower levels, still survive today.

A report in the Eckington Woodhouse & Stavely Express, dated 4th August 1899 shows a side-on picture of the mill on fire. The flames are shown reaching the threshold of the bridge, but being unable to leap the river. Common sense seems to say that a steam locomotive coming right into the mill, would itself represent something of a fire hazard, when you think of a papery environment, and the sparks emitted by the locos' of the period. In the very later years, a venerable old deisel shunter affectionately known as 'Blue Peter' did this work, driven by a jovial Irishman, Martin Casey. The brass air-horn of this engine was mounted and presented as a retirement present to Mr. B. Ashton, the yard foreman, when he left in 1983. In the few years following that the line was finally dismantled, having lasted for the best part of a hundred years.

Flooding was another spectre which haunted all South Yorkshire mills, built originally to make use of water wheels; and Spring Grove was no exception. Here a footbridge is in iminent danger of being swept away during a flooding of the Don just after the Second World War. It did actually break away moments after this picture was taken. Other incidents were far more devastating, though rarely captured on picture.

In the 1900s, this machine was called the 'Old Cutter'. It took in paper from three large rolls at the feed end to the left of the picture, trimmed it with one stroke, and let it fall into three piles on the flat platter visible on the right. This was then news-sheet size and ready for packing and dispatch. The fact that the machine was referred to as the old cutter, even then, could suggest that it dates from a time when the Dixons purchased such a machine from a bankrupt Ecclesfield paper firm, in the 1870s. This would make it a secondhand purchase, and hence even older than the 1870s. On

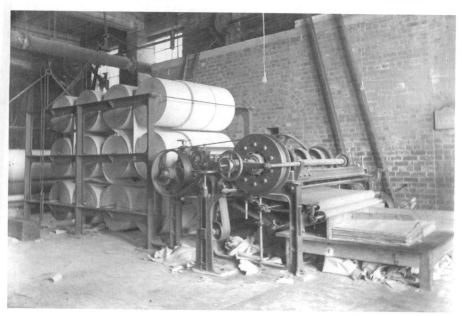

studying the photograph closely, the name 'Milton' appears to be embossed in the ironwork at the front. When looking through lists of UK patent applications, I found that a company called Milton took out patents for various kinds of leather cutting machinery and weaving looms in the 1850s and 60s. Since the earliest sites of the local paper industries had tended to be assembled in a piecemeal way, this machine may have been a version based on one of the loom or cutter patents, but modified after manufacture.

The appearance of a light bulb at the top of this 1906 picture is interesting. Electrical lighting in the 1900s was still not very widespread in use. It was only a couple of decades earlier that Thomas Edison had proved the possibility of lighting whole city districts in America with his own patent lighting apparatus. Gas mantles were still a strong mainstay of lighting at this time, both for domestic and industrial use. (with oil lamps still in use in this village). In this case however there was a very obvious safety precedent. Some loose paper from a roll came too close to a gas light fitting on the occasion of the mill's 1892 fire. This certainly rammed home the point that safety lighting is a must for a factory of this type.

This group of three lads had been photographed during a break, whilst sitting on the platter of the old cutter. They look to be around 14 years of age, so as this was then the starting age for youngsters, it would be safe to assume that they were relative newcomers to the mill. To be a young new starter in a 1900s paper mill meant, unless you were bound apprentice to a skilled occupation, that you were likely to be a broke-carrier and general 'sweeping-brush' worker. A fair amount of errand-running would probably be expected of you also, largely for dinners and drinks. When the owner previous to Dixon ran the mill, lads as young as nine were employed doing these general tasks. They were paid just a few shillings per week, 3 or 4 with a good employer, five if they were very lucky, and would work on towards more responsible tasks with experience and age.

The photographer, Mr. Robinson, did at one time spend some time working in this mill, so it comes as no surprise to find that some pictures of fellow workers, friends and neighbours from the village, at their posts, appear amongst this collection.

This picture was taken during alterations to the beater house. The white paper hats seen on some of the workmen were a distinctive feature of the paper mill, the idea being; "Why wear out your cloth cap at work, when you can make one out of the paper which is around in such abundance?" The man amongst the metal piping at top right is Billy Walker, and the lad at the top left of the picture is Frank Cauldwell.

The same group of workers can be seen here in a picture used by the firm in a commemorative book in later years. These men would have had various skills; those of plumbers, fitters, steel fabricators, carpenters, bricklayers and stonemasons. If all these skills were represented in one person, he would have been the firm's millwright at this time. But a look at the old Dixon pay ledgers surviving from the period shows that there were many different skills employed, scattered through quite a few people. This could have been because of all the repairs, additions and newbuild work that was taking place then, requiring more labourers than before. All the skilled men were overseen and organised as a team however, by two engineers Mr. Oliver and Mr. McRorie.

The machinery of the beater house had been destroyed in a disastrous fire near the turn of the century. The insurance arrangements however, had been very good, so all repair and replacement work went ahead swiftly, and was easily financed. An opportunity was taken to put in improved plant and machinery for this section after the 1899 fire, and that was running to capacity by 1910.

35

This room was called the 'Salle', although the way it was usually pronounced sounded more like "Sol". It was really one end of a long shed which which was the finishing dept'. The staff of this area comprised the men and women whose job it was to pack the bundles of paper for dispatch, in this case 'reams' of 500 sheets. A 'Printers ream' was 516. Unfortunately I haven't been able to track down anyone who knew or could recognise any of the lady employees in this picture. However I am told that the man standing at the far right is Mr. Wilfred Jackson, and the one at far left is Mr. Frederick Reid. Mr. Reid began work at the mill when the Marsh brothers were the owners, before 1871, and he worked there till his retirement in 1924. Such is the detail in this picture, direct from a glass negative taken in 1907, that we can see the bandaged thumb of the woman to the left of the group. It is possible to receive an injury like this from the sharp edge of a piece of paper strangely enough, and continuous production line handling made this a known hazard.

Here a group of mill working girls have gathered for a picture, possibly at the end of work. Their distinctive hats were seen in several groups around the firm in Edwardian times. I have heard that they wanted to outshine the 'pork-pie' hats worn by the men.

None of these girls seem to be named in account ledgers of the time, unlike the main body of the workforce. They seem to be referred to simply as 'Girls' or 'New Girls', next to a large combined wage figure, probably to be divided in a sub-ledger.

Still relatively close to the mill, this part of the main road in 1910 was a good place to view the low part of the village, with hilltop details stretching away up to the right, before the trees grew up to largely obscure the scene. The lean-to stone shed at the near end of the row of cottages was a filesmith's workshop, and it still stands to this day; although the windows are now blocked up. At the other end of that terraced row is Green Lane, the turnoff which leads up to the hill-top areas in the distance. The black and white woodwork of Spring Grove House, with its corner tower, can be seen looking out from Usher Wood. This house was like many other Victorian houses purchased by mill owners of the time, in that it was added to and embellished, to become the grandest house in its settlement. The side which faces us had a style which mimicked the houses of Tudor merchants in the 16th century. The other side had earlier influences. Only the gate house of Spring Grove now remains from the original grouping. Further up, and silhouetted on the skyline is 'Hill End House'. The photographer in this case was standing at the lower part of the school yard, where some steps lead down to the main road. The gas lamp was there to light the footpath which leads up to school lane.

Another small workshop could be found in Usher Wood. This one, a wooden-built one was a 'Haft' shop. that is to say it was connected with the knife making industries. It was owned by the Rhodes family, seen here taking a break from the daily 'graft' on what must have been a good summer's day; warm enough to sit out on the roof.

37

Here is pictured the workforce of Spring Grove Mill, at a time when it numbered 122 in total. This photograph was taken in mid-1926, whilst the General Strike was on. The

scene was just outside the parish hall in Oughtibridge, after what was apparently a large meeting of employees inside. Everyone is dressed in their best, and present are gardeners, chauffeurs and directors as well as the main mill workforce.

Seen here with a flower in his buttonhole, Mr. Dixon was in fact going through a difficult period in this year. He was providing newsprint for a special newspaper called the British Gazette; produced during the national emergency. No other news press was operating. The mill worked on through this time, whilst the rest of the country was virtually at a standstill. Consignments of newsprint were sent to the printing shop with outrider policemen literally hanging on to the outsides of the lorries. The danger of civil strife hung in the air for several months. Mr. Dixon had never had to face the idea of being a strike-breaker before.

Although the firm came through this episode seemingly unscathed, Joseph himself was affected by a sudden illness which overtook him towards Christmas of that year, and despite the efforts of hospital doctors, he died on the eighth of December. He was 77 years of age.

A group of workmen posed for this picture outside the Wharncliffe Arms. They were working on a new reservoir, which early in the 20th century was the Ewden Valley project. This is visible now as the More Hall reservoir, between Wharncliffe Side and Deepcar. Work began in 1913; and as the pub's signboard appears to be still the one used by Smith's 'Don Brewery', the picture must have been taken before the Tennant Brothers takeover in 1916. So we are looking at between 1913 and 1916. This pub and the Blue Ball provided workers victals for the men who passed on their way up the main road to the site of the dam. Many others actually lived on the site itself in a purpose made village, which had it's own canteen hall. The project went on until the late nineteen twenties. I have been told that the toddler in white at the left of the picture was Mary Dawson.

By the late 1950's when the view of the paper mill (over) had been taken 'Dixcel' paper had become a household name, and the factory was a well known landmark on this trunk route to Manchester. The old store sheds outside had been completely removed and replaced by a car shelter, which can be seen modestly parked up with a few old Austins, a Ford and two Morris Minors. Car owners, even as late as 1959, were still a minority amongst the workforce.

The old square chimney continued to reach towards the skyline, although it was soon to be accompanied by the round-built one familiar today, standing further back. The hillside behind the mill, then as now, was land belonging to the Earl of Wharncliffe's Estates, and was only thinly wooded compared with the covering it now has. This was because a branch of the Women's Land Army, the 'Timber Corps' had taken many of the sizeable pine trees to be used as pit props in Britain's mines during World War II. The dam building work took some sixteen years to complete, and drew in men from both Wharncliffe Side and Oughtibridge, at a time when people had to take on what

39

Spring Grove Paper Mill, in the late 1950s

labouring work they could wherever it appeared. Mr. Marsden, a farmer from Brightholmlee told me of days when he worked on the dam in the 1920s. An Oughtibridge man Mr. Len Elsdon (Senior). can be seen third from the right, on the

front row of this picture, about to start work along with his mates. Groups like this were hired on a short term basis to do the sweated labour of earth and rubble moving, although I have seen images of steam-powered excavators also in use at this site. A railway line was built from Wharncliffe Wood to the Ewden Valley site, crossing over the river Don and main road at More Hall. This was used to bring workers in and move the diggings and clay, as can be seen here, in trucks. Near the gates by the main road which now lead through to the reservoir, an embankment can still be seen where the railway bridge went over the road. The bridge over the river still stands too, but today is gated off.

More evidence of the reservoir work, and its knock-on effect can be seen here, in a picture of the Blue Ball Inn taken in 1917. The hanging ball is still there unchanged, but the building has been altered by discontinuing the use of the front stable, and converting it for saloon bar use. The door nearest to us, unlike the earlier picture, is no longer a stable door, but has been opened up for customer use. It has been given a smart marble-effect surround; like the far one, and its lintel now advertises 'Berry's Sparkling Ales'. A new landlord is here in residence, William Young, who took over at the start of the First World War. A dairy, which was in the yard off the left of the picture, continued working as

such for a good few years after this, dispite the changes that were taking place. As well as landlord and landlady there seems to be two women employees visible here, in the far doorway. This increase in bar staff would appear to tie in with the need for meals, and a bigger inside space to look after, following the influx of the reservoir workers. I am not sure what the occasion is here, but an open-topped cab is in attendance, with a driver and bowler-hatted groom, complete with a flower in his buttonhole. It may perhaps be a wedding reception which has drawn a few interested watchers.

On Langsett Road in Oughtibridge the Filesmith's Arms, a 'Cannon Ales' pub, took its name from the local workshop industry of making files, another of the 'Little Mester' skills practised in tiny, tucked away premises here and there. At present this building is the village grocers shop. At the far end was the newsagent shop, which to this day is still used as such. Back when this picture was taken, in 1907, the advertising signage it carried was made of enamelled sheets of iron, now sometimes referred to as 'street jewellery' and avidly sought by collectors. The prices of consumer goods in Edwardian times were so stable that they could be committed to the enamel of these signs, and left for a good few years with no change.

The figure of a forge worker, recognisable by his white sweat-cloth around his neck, can be seen standing at the junction with Bridge Hill. He was probably just up from Blackwell's by the river for a welcome midday break away from the heat.
The biggest employer in Oughtibridge was the Silica Brick Company, seen here in 1910, with its workings stretching up the hillside from Beely Wood towards

42

Wharncliffe Wood. Close to us is 'Low Yard' as it was called. The top yard can be seen higher up the hillside. Both yards had kilns in which the brick clay was fired to a hard consistency.

The Dyson Holmes Forge formerly called 'Holmes Steel Works' started life as a small works owned by Mr. George Dickinson. The earliest mention of it appears to be in a newspaper article of 1837, the "Leeds Intelligentsia", which describes the route of a famous fox hunt. By 1851 George Dickinson Junior had been recorded in the Census as the "Forgeman and Tilter" in residence, along with the names of his wife, children and four apprentices living on site.

At the close of the 19th century it was being operated by the cutlery manufacturer Joseph Rodgers & Sons Ltd. for the manufacture of 'Shear Steel'. The buildings seen on the right housed a furnace and two tilt hammers, along with the water wheel which drove them, and were situated against the retaining wall of a dam used to store a "head" of water for powering the wheel. The big stone blocks which make up this wall remain largely in place to this day, and one was even reinstated very recently.

After falling into disuse for a period at the start of the 20th century the site re-started as a hatchet making works in the 1920s, under the managership of a Mr. Percy Stringer. This is probably the time from which the photograph dates. Mr. Stringer had a previous history of hatchet manufacturing at the Niagara works at Wadsley Bridge, for a few years around 1916. Several local men have recounted, from their youth the day of Stringer's appearance at the Wharncliffe Schoolroom to ask if any of them, then in their final week of attendanc, aged 14, would be interested in starting their first Job at the tilt. Cyril Spooner, Ernest Charlesworth, Alfred Westwood, George Mortimer and Hedley Crawshaw were amongst those taking up the offer in the late '20s.

In this lull in a football 'kickabout' on Langsett Road Oughtibridge, we see a lineup of youngsters in the middle of a very clear street scene, dating from 1906. It is here too that we can see more about everyday occupations in the village. To the left we can see a cab business, 'E. Morton; Cab Proprietor', and Mr. Morton is standing outside his shop, close to the kids. A Saddler by the name of J. Dyson has the premises next to him. These two occupations had similar skills where it came to preparing a horse for human transportation; so it was mutually helpful for them to exist close to each other. The businessmen of this rural north-of town district tended to function in co-operation rather than in rivalry.

In the distance is a very clear view of Haywards the butchers, 'Purveyers of Home Cured Hams and Bacon'. John Hayward's shop, with its large wooden hood at the front, keeping the direct sun off the meat, was quite a grand building as butchers shops go of the time. In addition to the ground floor shop, and abbatoir at the  rear, there was a sizeable upper room in which functions and meetings were sometimes held.

The newsagent's shop to the right of the picture is still as such now. Behind the wagon at far left of this scene is the doorway of Micklethwaite's hardware and paraffin shop. Villagers came here to buy their lamp fuel and wicks; candles too when needed. The wooden building with its window propped open was a fish and chip shop.

Some 35 years later, this street hadn't changed very much at all. We are now in the early nineteen forties, during World War 2. A truck and motorcycle can be seen on the road, rare in 1906, but by now more commonplace. The chip shop has been demolished and a petrol pump stands on the spot. In the yard, set back from the pump was a garage owned by the Cooperative Society. By this time the paraffin shop had been taken over by the Parkin family, and was known locally as the 'tintack shop'.

A welcome sight in the end wall of Cherry Tree Row was Fletcher's bread and cakes shop, run by William and Clara Fletcher. This was a favourite haunt of Oughtibridge youngsters, not least for the mouthwatering smells which wafted out on to the pavement at baking times. Here a fresh loaf could be bought; plain and current tea cakes, buns, tarts, biscuits and scrumptious Eccles cakes. Herbert took this picture on a clear sunny day in 1907.

Mrs Fletcher also made ice cream, selling it at 1d a glass. There are villagers who still to this day say that they have not tasted ice cream as good as Clara Fletcher's. Grandchildren in the family can remember being collared to do the job of turning the ice cream churner, seemingly endlessly, to produce the shop's supply. Fresh milk needed for this would have come from one of the hill farms; of which there were several locally, and eggs came from just across the yard, off the right hand side of the picture, where one of Clara's sons kept poultry. The downstairs side window which faces us is where the kitchen was. Home-made pickles, black puddings and pork pies could be bought at this shop too. Husband William, as well as being the proprieter named above the shop, also worked at the nearby Silica Firebrick works.

Just a few yards on from the bread shop was Oughtibridge Post Office. Here we see the Unwin family, with Mr. and Mrs Unwin standing in the doorway of the shop. Lydia Unwin was the postmistress. The couple's daughter Sybil was the daytime telephone operator at the exchange in Orchard Street. The shop window into which the other two young Unwins are leaning was a recent addition at the time this photograph was taken, around 1912. A large GPO parcel basket can be seen just inside the garden gateway. From here a barrow was wheeled every day all the way up to the station to meet the mail-carrying train. Incoming mail for the village would then be exchanged for outgoing. In later years the post office moved to Bridge Hill.

John Hayward's 'Family Butcher' business was a main focal point of the village at the time that this photograph was taken in 1907, as indeed it was for almost all the time it stood. Villagers of the depression years later on can remember it being used, not only as the shop, but also as a casual impromptu meeting place. Unemployed men would stand under the wooden hood, known locally as the 'Shed', and either wait for the postmaster to emerge on Bridge Hill with a telegram for someone to deliver; a job typically worth 6d, or just stand and chat. If the group got to a size such that it spilled out from the

46

pavement on to the road, one of their number would take on the self-appointed task of directing traffic around the gathering. He would be called the 'Chocolate Bobby' for that particular day. Local carols were known to be struck up here at the festive season, an arrangement whereby revellers would meet under the canopy at a certain time on Christmas night each year. The familiar strains of 'Jacob's Well' or 'Good News' would then be heard drifting through the night-time streets, as a seemingly perfect end to the day.

On ordinary days Mary Elsdon remembers being sent to Hayward's to get a 'tuppenny bag' of "Blue-Bits", last parings from the bones, useful for making stews, soups and pies enough for a week and more, for a family of six. To the right of the picture, the iron railings visible near the woman in white marks the place where, in later years the doorway to the village's public library was. Two floors higher, where the projecting attic dormers can be seen, several rooms were made into flats and rented out. These were still in use as late as 1970.

As a smaller kind of group picture, this gathering of 7 Silica Brick employees has a 'pally' kind of feel to it which is sometimes absent from the larger workforce group pictures. It was taken in 1916, at a time when already some of the brickyard employees had been drawn into the first great offensives of the Great War. At far left is Bill Woodhead. Then the three ladies standing closest to him are Victoria Housley front left, Cecilia Housley next to her, and Amy Housley just behind him. The man in the middle of the group isn't known. The girl at the very top of the group is Annie Kirk, and the last man at far right is Ted Hurst. Behind the group is the 'Jinny' line, which was in effect a long cable driven in a continuous loop by an engine. Small trucks running on rails and loaded with diggings were hitched to the line at intervals, so that they could be pulled along, with the full ones going in one direction, and the emptied ones in the other. The man in charge of the winding engine was paid £1. 5s and 6d per week in the 1920s. The trench system through which the rails ran can still be found in Wharncliffe Wood, with some fragments of rail, sleepers and iron wheels still in evidence too.

This business made use of seams of Ganister, a kind of gritty hard stone found under layers of low grade coal and shale respectively (never very deep down). For many years it had been known that if this stone was crushed into powder and then incorporated into clay, it was possible to make bricks with a high fire-resistant quality.

EUROPEAN WAR, 1914.

Yorkshire Silica Fire Brick Works,
OUGHTIBRIDGE, NEAR · SHEFFIELD.

Roll of Honour

STAFF & EMPLOYEES WHO HAVE JOINED HIS MAJESTY'S FORCES.

Hanley Brooke	Jno. Whitham	J. Betts	C. Bradshaw	A. Dutton
F. W. Brooke	E. Collins	H. Hawley	J. Wood Jr.	D. Savoury
Allen Brittison	A. Hoyle	G. F. Hawley	H. Holmes	A. Eccles
F. W. Hodger	Geo. Hill	J. W. Whiteley	H. Haigh	W. Coldwell
W. Bramwell	G. F. Ormrod	C. Gardner	Gr. Whiteley	H. Whitham
F. R. Brooke	F. Marsh	G. H. Collett	Jno. Armitage	C. Gould
H. Brooke	G. Masley	A. Jarrett	Saml. Taylor	H. Gould
Chas. Ashton	J. Ashforth	H. Hector	W. Hirst	A. J. Gould
A. Barnes	J. D. Crofts	J. C. Salmon	Geo. Rushton	L. Quickfall
H. Beever	H. Nettleton	G. H. Watson	P. Hershaw	A. Armitage
J. H. Clark	W. Owen	G. W. Barker	C. Bewell	J. E. Bohm
W. Beever	Wm. Whiteley	F. Marsden	D. Hallam	D. Mellor
H. Beadson	Chas. Marsh	C. Littlewood	A. Helliwell	Albt. Carr
J. H. Eccles	Wm. Whitham	G. Henshaw	Jno. Smith	G. Armitage
R. Taylor	Jno. Dyson	R. Woodhead Jr.	H. Horton	J. Jenkinson
Am. Lutterill	F. Thompson	A. Jones	J. Spilling	W. Ashall
Jno. Rodgers	E. Yeardley	H. Beresford	W. Skelton	L. Minnis
E. S. Woodcock	G. Garnett	W. Hawley	W. Parrott	C. Hobson
W. Bacon	J. Drousfield	J. D. Oxfield	J. Robinson	W. Ashforth
A. Whitham	F. Peer	G. Butlies	W. Severn	P. Austin

EXPLANATIONS:— ✚ Killed. ∗ Wounded. ‡ Prisoner. ◦ Discharged.

The steel furnaces and refractories of Sheffield and elsewhere needed large quantities of these bricks, as did the kilns of the pottery industries, for linings.

The amount of ganister taken and used reached a peak just after the turn of the century; 40,000 tons in 1908. This business and the nearby paper mill were the main two employers of the area, but it was always reckoned that a move to the paper mill was a move up the ladder, in terms of pay and conditions for the worker who could achieve that move. For one thing the blasting process used to extract the ganister caused respiratory diseases.

The First World War took its toll of the Silica workers, as the roll of honour shows. This was printed before the hostilities had ceased, and records wounded and missing men as well as those killed. In the Oughtibridge area some lads as young as sixteen were known to have attempted to join up in the early years of high nationalistic enthusiasm.

Here was one of the Oughtibridge 'Drifts'; tunnels dug into the hillside in a direction chosen to meet a vein of the mineral the miners were after. As the mineral was worked out, the mine got deeper. They were lined with stonework or bricks for the first few yards, and the diggings were taken out along the rail in small trucks called 'corves'. These rail trackways were around for use like this even before the industrial revolution had started, and certainly pre-dated the idea of railways for transporting people. Once inside, the miners would take the work deeper and deeper into the hillside, propping up the roof with wooden beams as they went. Side tunnels would branch off from the main 'drive' to seek for the valuable mineral; some would go quite a distance, some only a few yards.

One of the miner's main fears, that of flooding, was mercifully easier to deal with in this kind of mine because drainage tunnels or 'soughs' could be dug to link up with the drift from lower down the hill. Any water near the workfaces would then be allowed flow away via gravity before serious buildup occurred. This effectively did away with the need for a pumping engine. It has been said that drift mines were cheaper to operate because of that particular advantage. Deep mines, reached by a vertical shaft were not so blessed, and could often be plagued by floodwater.

A typical set of axle & wheels, which was part of one of the corves used in Wharncliffe Wood. This one was found in the 1990s.

Evidence of stone quarrying can be found in a number of places in the village; Owler Gate, the hill-top areas of Spout House and Bent Hill, the 'Rocher', as it is locally called, and at Glen Howe. Stone from the Wharncliffe Crags was used to build the railway bridge in the Wicker in Sheffield, which carries a date-stone of 1839. Most of the quarrying here however was for local purposes i.e. for houses and farm buildings, dry stone walls and drinking troughs for the animals. Two wiers span the river Don in the village, made from locally quarried blocks. Square holes can be seen in them where iron bars were keyed in as a means to moving them around. Large blocks of a similar millstone grit can be found also at the Dyson Holmes Tilt. These held back the waters of a small dam for driving a water wheel. At two different locations along the length of Tinker Brook I myself have come across examples of worn-down, discarded grinding wheels. One indeed is set in the stone floor of what remains of one of the workshops, still visible at the tilt just mentioned. Several of these wheels carry the marks of the grinder's periodic attempts to 'true-up' the spin of the stones, following uneven wear.

Here an unfinished stone trough can be seen still attached to the large rock base from which it was carved, at a hill-top quarry on the edge of the village. A split had opened up on the far corner, forcing the workman to abandon it all those years ago. It must have been a black day for him having got thus far, then having to leave it, as stone cutting was a work of sweat and graft, as much as skill. Here we can see a two-horse team pulling a mechanical reaper during the oats harvest, one of the last harvests of the farming year, in a picture taken in 1905. The scene is a field belonging to Bitholmes Farm, which was the property of the Grayson family at this time.

Before the advent of horse-drawn mechanical reapers and reaper/binders, much of this work was done with scythes and sickles. The men used the scythes, and women the sickles. Harvest time was very much a family affair. Parents and elder family heads would typically be seen at the front of a team making low, sweeping cuts into the crop as they moved foreward. Youngsters would follow up behind with gathering, binding and stooking. Alongside that team would be another, probably representing another family. The bigger fields would be likely to require several overlapping teams, to create a broad front, at reaping time.

Oats was known to be easier to cut than wheat or barley, so Elias Grayson, shown here with his combined scythe and cradling attachment; to catch sheaf-sized bundles, would have been able to make fairly swift headway through a field in his prime years. It was reckoned that a reaper, equipped with a good scythe could cut two acres (0.8 ha) per day. On a good day, work would only be interrupted by the application of the sharpening stone to the underside of the blade, and the welcomed meal at noon.

Cornmill Cottage was one of three working cornmills in the area, the others being Mr. Jarvill's mill off Church St. Oughtibridge, and one on

51

Wheel Lane Oughtibridge. It could be found at the bottom of the lane which starts by the Wharncliffe Arms pub. Here, close to the river, a water wheel turned heavy machinery in the taller building visible to the left, and ground wheat down into flour and bran husk. The water which turned the wheel came from a goit which ran largely underground from a sluice by the wier just up-river. The miller who lived here at the turn of the century was Henry Charlesworth. A line of large stepping stones made it possible to cross the river Don at a point near the cottage, and these survived for many years after the mill ceased working.

Another sight of the cornmill could be acquired by taking the popular "long" view from the lofty position of Crag-View, as here in a photograph taken in 1906. The Ordinance Survey map of some fifty years previous to this shows that the goit, having fed water to this mill continued on to supply a grinding hull (recently rediscovered), and then lastly the dam used by the paper mill further down the river. The notion of all three mills being once in the same owner's hands is strongly hinted at in this sharing of the same water supply, and the fact that they all, at one time, carried the same name. A glance at that 1855 map reveals that they were each called Spring Grove. The one pictured here was differentiated simply by having the word 'Corn' in brackets added to the title Spring Grove Mill. The grinding hull was called 'Spring Grove Wheel'.

Transport

Whatever may be said about the quality of the main road through Wharncliffe Side in the early 1900s, the fact is that there wasn't much to be had by way of transport in the 1900s, for a villager, apart from his or her own two feet. Indeed people did walk the seven miles into Sheffield and the three miles to Stocksbridge for trade, to visit, or simply to buy something which was not available locally. This was the accepted way of life and people had never known things any different.

Before the coming of the turnpikes movement relied largely on the pack-horse tracks which criss-crossed the countyside. These tended to cling to the high places, so that travellers could see and recognise the places they were approaching from the advantage of altitude. However, the way they simply followed the landcape, with little or no concept of the straight, level and smooth, ruled out all but the hardiest of wheeled vehicles. Pack animals i.e. horses and donkeys loaded with 'carrier' trade items, led by people hardened and familiar with the hazzards of the routes were amongst the few users. In Wharncliffe Side the main road when it came, was constructed to the west of the river and alongside it, in a gradual climb from Sheffield; so that in the centre of the village it reaches 600 ft above sea level.

Although railways had superceded the horse as the mainstay of transport between cities in the 19th century, horses remained ubiquitous as a localized form of carriage for people and goods at this time. It has been estimated that in late Victorian times one horse for every ten people was the figure needed to keep society going. The coal man, milk man, brewer's drayman, all delivered by horse. Agriculture still ran largely by the pull of horses, and shops were supplied by horse-drawn vans. Horse population continued to rise, and reached a peak in 1902 of three and a half million. In an ironic twist, the decline which followed has recently been reversed, thanks to the growth of leisure equestrianism, and now stands far in excess of that 1902 figure, even though modern society has long since ceased to depend on our four legged friend.

Here a waggoner and his team of horses has come to rest at one end of 'Saw Pit Row',

a row of cottages along the main road, just a little way down from the Blue Ball Inn. The dwellings to the left have in recent years been renovated. This picture has come to be known as 'Winter Delivery'. The driver is Mr. Harry Littlewood, ('Flash Harry') and the lad holding the 'chain' horse is John Leggitt. A chain horse, sometimes known as a 'cock-horse' was a helping addition which was often added to the front of pulling teams, temporarily, in hilly districts. Such a horse was stabled at the Cock Inn in Oughtibridge, for use on waggons as they passed through if needed; especially for the eastwards or westwards journies. This conferred on the pub its name.

The lane almost directly across from the row of cottages in this picture, Dyson Holmes Lane, was particularly steep where it joined on to the main road; as it still is now. The firm which used it, Joseph Rodgers & Sons, owners of the forge at the bottom, had repeated difficulty, as George Dickinson had before, in getting wagonloads of shear steel up to reach the main road. They often needed a chain horse.

The road itself was the Wadsley to Langsett Turnpike road, which was constructed in 1806. The traveller who didn't have a horse, or any horse-drawn transport, generally speaking would have to walk. It was possible to catch a horse-drawn omnibus into Sheffield just before the turn of the century, but there was only one per week, leaving from outside the Blue Ball Inn at 7pm on Sundays. A motor bus wasn't available through this area till 1912, and even this only went down as far as Middlewood, to the start of the original tram lines. If you didn't want to walk, you could cycle. There were a good half dozen bicycle manufacturers in Sheffield at this time; names like John Watchhorn, F.H. Anderton, and Hydes & Wigfull. A good sound bicycle however could cost between six and nine pounds, and not many local people belonged to an income group which could cover such an amount lightly. For the rich, there was the motor car.

This was Mr. Blowers, the chauffeur for Spring Grove House, and the car which he drove for the Dixon family was a Napier, 6 cylinder, 30 horse-power car. This was the four seater 'Tourer' model of 1907. The 'W' on the registration plate tells us that the vehicle was registered in Sheffield and, from the overall appearance, the car seems to be quite new. This has led to the speculation that the picture was taken in 1907 or 1908. It was obviously springtime at the 'Big House', because a bed of flowering tulips can be seen in the right-hand background of the picture. The cost of petrol at this time was 7d a gallon, and the speed limit had just been raised to 20 mph. The compulsary registration of cars had only been in existance for 5 years, and many of the motoring laws which we take for granted nowadays, including the compulsary driving test, were still many years away.

Here the paper mill steam lorry, loaded with a consignment of newsprint paper, is taking a brief pause before setting off to its customer destination. With driver and stoker sitting on either side of the central boiler, it is waiting on a stretch of road across from the mill's main entrance, tucked in under the Crag-View cliffs. It is probably at this moment that the time-keeper Charles Slater, the man leaning on the wagon, has checked the contents of the load with an inventory in his hand. The driver would probably carry a version of this too, as a delivery note

The wagon itself is a five ton Coulthard steam lorry, manufactured in Preston, Lancs'. Available evidence from its registration number puts its time of manufacture at the years 1904/5. Because the vehicle appears quite new, this would probably date the picture to around that time too. Steam haulage wagons that were registered in the West Riding of Yorkshire were all given the prefix of 'C'. It seems that another firm which had ownership of this wagon during Edwardian times was Stainsby & Lyons Ltd. of Knottingly, a firm of tar distillers and chemical manufacturing. The single headlamp at the front was lit by acetylene gas, and the two-tiered steering wheel was in fact a combined steering wheel and regulator. The upper wheel was for steering and the lower one, effectively, was the throttle. A large tank of water stood on the opposite side of the road from the area pictured, a few hundred yards back from the rear of the vehicle. This contained enough water to refill the wagon's boiler several times over; which was handy on the occasions when several return journeys had to be made in one day.

The fleet of haulage vehicles (over) was the business which belonged to Harold Morton, son of the cab proprieter Eli Morton. At the time this picture was taken, in the mid 1920s, it numbered some half dozen assorted pickup trucks, flatbed trucks and at least one charabanc. Seen here from the left is an A.E.C., then a Shefflex truck, followed by a Daimler charabanc and another A.E.C. Finally a 'Bullnosed' Morris Cowley car is parked sideways on, Harold's family vehicle. The gentlemen

accompanying the vehicles are, from the left:- Billy Morton, Alec Morton, Herbert Hague, a young Walter Ibbotson, Roland James, Douglas Morton, Arnold Beaver, Harry Skelton, Harold Morton, Mr. Aliban, an unknown man, and finally Mr. Bagnall. The hill we are on is Church Street, at a point where a right turnoff can be taken which leads to a yard. It was from there that the vehicles had emerged to line up for the picture. The yard was shared between Harold's haulage business and Charles Jarvill the flour miller. The corner building in the centre of this picture was converted into a shop shortly after the picture was taken, a greengrocers, also run by the Morton family.

Shefflex trucks were the product of the Sheffield Simplex Motor Company, makers of luxury cars since the 1900s. They were sometimes referred to as the Sheffield Rolls Royce. By the mid-20s however there was little or no market for this kind of car, so the company had to shift over to the production of a workaday commercial vehicle in order to survive. It is thought that they used the experience they gained when designing a hardwearing and rugged chassis for armoured cars and ambulances during the First World War. The result turned out to be a durable and tough hauler for the '20s', with elliptical spring front suspension, solid tyres, a wooden cab with 'C' shaped side windows, and an optional tipping mechanism available for the back. The engines had a reputation for being vibration-free because of the precision with which the crankshafts were engineered; with emphasis on balance. The name Shefflex then replaced Simplex and carried on with great success. It survives even now in the Hillfoot area of the city, as a commercial trailer and coachbuilding firm.

In this incident, what appears to be a Sheffield Simplex car, the open-topped tourer model of 1908, had been travelling in the direction of Sheffield on the main road through the village. At a point just outside the Wharncliffe Arms pub it unfortunately shed it's nearside rear wheel. The driver can be seen staying with the car whilst help presumably was being sought. He looks a little worried, compared with the smiling faces of the children, who have gathered around with great interest. The cottages visible behind the car have been demolished in recent years, and replaced with newer housing following the same line. This scene was one of early days for the Simplex. The company had only just opened its factory under that name at Tinsley in 1907.

The advertisements of the period made much of the appeal attached to the rounded radiator design of Simplex's early cars. The price of £695 marked here (over) would not have been enough to purchase the open-topped touring version in the photo. That car carried the princely price tag of £855 in 1908.

"Sheffield-Simplex" Distinctiveness.

1. THE RADIATOR.

The Sheffield-Simplex radiator is not only distinctive and pretty—but it is also good. The design (registered), instead of following that of the ordinary flat-fronted radiator, is convex, and besides harmonising with the general appearance of the car, is of such proportions as to provide for an unusually large and effective cooling surface—a point which contributes, in no small degree, to the splendid efficiency of the engine.

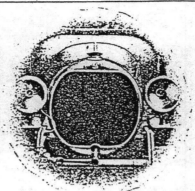

SHEFFIELD SIMPLEX

MADE IN SHEFFIELD WHERE THE STEEL COMES FROM.

"COUNTRY LIFE."
says :—

"Has a striking appearance on account of its novel radiator."

"LAND & WATER"
says :—

"It is a most difficult thing imaginable to design a new and attractive shape of radiator—there are already so many different kinds—but the new radiator of the Sheffield-Simplex is of exceptionally handsome appearance and distinctive design."

30 H.P.
6-CYLINDER
CHASSIS
£695
(Including 5 detachable Wire Wheels.)

Govt. Tax - £8 8 0

A catalogue will *interest*—but a trial will *convince* you. Both are free.

SHEFFIELD-SIMPLEX MOTOR WORKS, LTD.,
20, CONDUIT STREET, BOND STREET, LONDON, W.

Telegrams : "Shefflex, London." Works : Tinsley, Sheffield. Telephones: 6210 and 6211 Mayfair.

School Days

In the year of Queen Victoria's golden jubilee 1887, a national school was built in Wharncliffe Side. Amongst the people who contributed towards its building were Joseph Dixon of Spring Grove Mill and George Dickinson, the man who's father set up the tilt forge at Dyson Holmes. It was a mixed school, built originally to hold 120 children, although the average attendance at the turn of the century was 80.

This picture was taken on April 23rd 1908, when the school had only been standing for 21 years. As can be seen there were some late hill snows in that year. A wall divided the playground into two halves, so that the girls used the half which faces us, whilst the boys used the one at the other side.

In this picture, looking at the same side, we can see the square block which was the girl's cloakroom. A similar one at the other side was for the boys. In those days the children had to line up to have their shoes inspected for cleanliness before they were allowed in from the playground. The bell tower, used for calling everyone in for classes is visible here. This was dismantled in the 1960s.

In another 1908 picture, taken when the snow had gone, the sheds at the west end of the yard can be seen, which were the outside conveniences; again divided by the wall, so that there were three for the girls and two for the boys. School Lane can be seen curving over from left to right, behind the building, to join on to the main road.

This picture shows a class of pupils at a time not long after the school was built. The woman at the right hand end of the group is a pupil/teacher Lilly Senior, and at the left hand end is Miss Whitworth who was the official schoolmistress. It was not uncommon in those days for girl pupils to stay on to teach at their schools after their leaving age had passed.

By 1931 when this picture was taken the school honours board had recorded several generations of classroom achievers. In this case the 'County Minor' scholarship honours had gone to four pupils, Albert Paget the lad sitting on the ground, Kathleen Beaumont the girl sitting behind him, Kenneth Charlesworth the lad to the left of the board and Gwynneth Brooke the girl to the right. The school headmaster at this time was Mr. Woodcock, seen seated on the right.

Characters

Characters are what really make a village, and back in the 1900s they gave atmosphere, colour, allure and ultimately, reputation to an area. They frequently had direct influence over a family's desire to move from one region to another, just as did availability of work, features of landscape, climate, housing & schools etc., because good fellowship was important in the more isolated communities then.

Knicknames were liberally given out, based on the character, appearance or occupation of an individual; and they wouldn't fall shy of becoming personal in nature. Someone who was cheerful and sprightly could be known as 'Spriggy', someone who appeared to have a large mouth would be called 'Mussy'. Other local knicknames included 'Cash', 'Cheesey', 'Greno', 'Snecker', 'Doggie' and so on. This last name was given for no other reason that if you met the man on the street he would invariably have a small terrier dog protruding from the pocket of his large overcoat, indicating that he was on his way to a field of rabbit warrens. As you spoke with him the dog would simply watch you, and wouldn't be referred to in conversation at all. The photographer who took most of the pictures we are seeing was himself known as 'Spicy' Robinson, and Luther Fairest was known as 'Putty' Fairest because of his other occupation of repairing windows. To write about the origins of these and the many other names which made up the circle of familiarity would take up more than one book. Suffice to say however, that a chapter on some of them ought to be included as part of the early records of a village, whilst a memory of them still exists.

Here we see Mr. John Mills, known locally as 'Cocky' Mills, in the pleasant grounds of his glen. He is listed in the Kelly's Directory of 1893 as the proprieter of 'Glen Howe Pleasure Grounds', which he then ran on a commercial basis. He is standing about half way along the park's lower footpath, beside the brook, which is known as Tinker Brook. This was spanned by several rustic bridges, one of which is included here. The year is 1907. Mr Mills was said to have acquired the knickname 'Cocky' because of his intolerance of the more mischievous lads of the village, whom he tended to chase away when they fished in the brook ponds by his house.

Ten years after the picture was taken the park and its lands were gifted to the public in a generous move taken jointly

between Mr. Dixon, the local mill owner, and Mr. Mills. In the summer of 1917 an announcement appeared in the local newspaper saying that the park was about to be handed over to public use for ever. A firm of solicitors Messrs' Young & Wilson of East Parade, Sheffield had suggested that the local council, Wortley Rural District Council, could acquire the park for the public to use. It was intimated that Mr. J. Dixon was ready to put up a sum of £375, exactly half the buying price, if the council would put up the other half. The reply from the council was that it had no funds for such a purpose. However a friend of Mr. Dixon stepped in and offered the balance of the price. This was a man who wished to remain anonymous. Whoever he was, this was a very kind and generous thing to do, as Glen Howe has been a much used, admired and appreciated walkway, with much the same layout now as when it was gifted. One of the conditions of this handover was that Mr. Mills be allowed to remain in the tower house and live there as long as he liked. In the event however he didn't stay, but chose to move out and live somewhere else close-by, thus allowing the first publicly employed park keeper to take residence.

Some unforgettable characters were involved in the rescue of this local much-loved landmark. Glen Howe's pack horse bridge, formerly called 'New Mill' pack horse bridge, was brought from the village of Ewden, where it had been standing since 1734, as part of the well-worn route from Brightholmlee to Bolsterstone. This stone-by-stone move was one of the ideas aired and discussed initially by Joseph Dixon in his later years. After he died, his family carried out his wishes by completing the move. This happened just before the old valley and village of Ewden, along with the cottage in the picture, disappeared beneath the waters of the new reservoir in the late 1920s. Now the bridge spans Tinker Brook as part of the footpath in the upper part of Glen Howe,

where the brook enters the park. This is something of an ornamental retirement, when you think of the everyday hammering it would have had from hooves and cartwheels in the eighteenth century. There is a poem which records the knicknames of the villagers who's skills were used in the rescue of the bridge.

The Bridge in Glen Howe

The story of which I am going to relate
Is concerned with the bridge whose fame is great.
In six men's hands the work was done.
And down in history their names will run.

There's Nott Whittam of White Hart fame,
To run for the beer he is always game.
And Doggie Ridgewell is one who uses his wit,
He makes them laugh till their sides split.

Ted Hurst is a man with a big appetite,
And for him there's never too much to put out of sight.
Greno Fleetwood I think has missed his vocation,
The language he speaks are wonderful creations.

What a wonderful time piece Sammy Clarkson has got,
It will tell you the time right on the dot.
Then comes Jack Brooke, who is always dry,
After a few pints he makes the work fly.

To hear these men talk you never can tell,
Which is the boss for they all know it well.
So when in Glen Howe this bridge you see,
Take off your hats to these great men with me,
For the wonderful work they all have done.

J. 'Doggie' Ridgewell

The tower house was John's home since he bought the estate and had it built at the start of the 1880s. The park itself is a deep, wooded ravine with a brook running through the bottom, and winding walks leading eventually to a clearing at the top of the south slope. The swings, roundabout and rocking horse occupied this field/clearing for many years. Recently a circular stone enclosure was built there by an organisation known as 'South Yorkshire Forest', as part of a Wharncliffe Side and Oughtibridge area heritage trail project. The tower nestles in the lower part of the glen, not far from the park entrance. Recently it has had to undergo some structural repairs, and, as local people will remember, the tea room beside it was

dismantled in the mid-1970s. The photographer was standing on the ground which rises behind the tower to take this 1905 picture, in an area which was set aside for the work of cutting and dressing stone. Mr. Mills, as well as running the park, quarried stone from his glen. This was a smallish operation however, and the little quarries in Glen Howe were known as stone 'Pits', as were some similar ones higher up the hillside at Owler Gate.

On entering the park, the deep natural cutting takes walkers alongside Tinker Brook in an upstream direction, leading them eventually to the high part where the oldest trees are. The meandering paths provide multiple routes for this, on either side of the brook, and several footbridges are there to assist. John Mills used the stone from his quarries to create pools of running water on several levels, similar to the way that

the local mills stored and layered their 'heads' of water for use on water wheels. There were stepped cascades, and a straight fall of water near to the tower, put there to keep the interest of visitors in the refreshment area. For many years it has been possible to peer over a rustic fence, into the drop of the fall, and see shoals of trout when the sun shines down into the lower pool.

Amongst the visitors to the park in the early years of the twentieth century were groups of underprivileged schoolchildren, sometimes 350 at a time, who were given the opportunity to travel up from the poorer city areas, and enjoy the park by way of a charitable fund known as the 'Fresh Air Fund'. This cause had been run from its earliest times, by a co-operation between two men, Arthur Pearson, who owned the magazine 'Pearson's Weekly', and John Kirk, a man known for his work as secretary of the 'Ragged School Union'. These special trips, by train up to Oughtibridge station, then on foot to Glen Howe, were greatly looked foreward to and heartily enjoyed. Teachers supervised the children, and kept them in manageable groups. By the time they reached the tower there was, on each occasion, a big picnic tea waiting for them by arrangement.

The old tea pavilion here was one that preceded the tea room which most villagers will remember. Its wooden sides were constructed in a series of arches, and on the whole, the building looked quite pleasant, complementing the tower and inviting walkers to take rest and refreshment. A wooden sign jutted out at one end, itself forming an arch. This read; 'Glen Howe Tower: Teas and Hot Water Provided. Large or Small Parties. Lowest Charges.' The final part of the sign, barely legible, said; 'Cigars Etc., and Blend.' (meaning 'blend' pipe tobacco). During research I met people who could remember the pre-1917 days in the park when 'Old John' prepared teas and ham sandwiches, using his own home-cured hams, and his son who was also called John, served them up into the tea room.

The park really came alive when the schoolchildren arrived. A long line of cups of tea was distributed in an orderly way, and then each pupil went on to get a tea-cake. They would next go up into the top field to play various games, which included rounders and cricket. To come from the grimy industrial city to this was a heaven for the kids. Nowadays, with travel for everyone taken pretty much for granted, it is difficult for us to imagine a people so held back as to need a benevolent fund just to be able to see green open spaces.

Mr. Mills once had the honour of welcoming a world famous character to the park. Colonel William F. Cody, 'Buffalo Bill' had brought his wild west show from the US to tour Britain just after the turn of the century. Bill took time off from the 1903 Sheffield venue simply to view the park, which it was said he greatly admired. After an enjoyable day visiting with John, he was said to have used his two Colt Peacemakers to shoot his initials into a tree.

The man we saw leaning on the steam lorry earlier was Charles Slater. Seen here on the left of this twosome, Charles's unusual feature, not immediately obvious, was that he only had one arm. His left arm, always skillfully

posed in photographs as resting by his side, hand in pocket, was a false one. The loss of his own arm came about through a mill accident which happened in the very early part of his working life; evidently at a brick-making works in Deepcar. At the time this photograph was taken Charles was the time-keeper at Spring Grove Mill. The handicap didn't appear to have stopped him from being an active musical director and conductor of the chapel band, with a loyal following of instrumentalists.

67

Worship

Wharncliffe's Wesleyan chapel, set squarely beside the main road, has been the local place of worship through the best part of two hundred years now. It was built in 1807, at more or less the same time as the road itself was being constructed, as the local turnpike. There has been a traditional idea in the village that before this chapel was available, a small chapel existed in the little hamlet of Brightholmlee, which is a settlement of very old stone dwellings on the hillside behind the site. Some small pieces of evidence have been found which partially support this. It seems more likely however that part of a cottage would have been allocated for use, from time to time, as a place of worship. Certainly the name 'Wharncliffe Side', as a village did not exist in 1807, and the whole area was known as Brightholmlee, even amongst the furthest scattered farms and cottages, till well into the 19th century. It was the crag side of the valley which carried the name of Wharncliffe at those earlier times.

This is how the Brightholmlee Methodist Chapel appeared circa 1905, when it was nearly a hundred years old, in a picture taken by Luther Fairest. It was made from locally quarried stone, and the purchase of the land on which it stands was handled, in the negotiating stages, by Thomas Holy, a personal friend of John Wesley. The land originally belonged to a man called John Helliwell, and it was known as the 'Great Horse Close'. The document relating to the sale measures two and a half feet by two feet, and it records all the names of those involved in the setting up of the chapel in the valley, around ten people in all. These were very self-reliant folks, locals all, and they appear to have put up the building themselves with little or no outside help. So many of the old stone buildings of Wharncliffe Side seem to date from just after 1807, that it seems reasonable to suggest that the coming of the chapel was a trigger to the first growth years of the village. After that there was definitely a recognisable core to the settlement, the shape of which is still visible now.

The datestone above the chapel door was readable at the time this photograph was taken. Today it is largely weathered away. As well as recording the date of erection, 1807, it carried a sobering message; 'Prepare to meet thy GOD', from chapter four of the Old Testament Book of Amos. Such fire and brimstone messages were not uncommon in the early meetings that John Wesley set up at the birth of the movement. Methodism got its name from the way it regulated the lives of the founding members. In Oughtibridge from the 1880s the Rev. W. Rowthorne gave some chastening sermons about what he saw as a spiritual and moral lapse then redolent in the activity of 'drinking on Sundays'. However, this kind of Evangelical worship was also very profound and heart-stirring. Wesley's brother Charles wrote many hymns for the movement which show genuine poetic feeling, such as 'Love divine all Love's excelling', 'Jesu, lover of my soul', and the Christmas Carol 'Hark the herald angels sing'. The 'Amos' message also featured in the decorations on pottery items made in Yorkshire from 1820-30. This type of pearlware pottery, occasionally seen adorning people's homes in the form of wall-plates and display-crockery, was often called 'Pious Ware'.

In spring and summer sometimes, services would be conducted in the open air, like as here at School Farm at 'Anniversary'. This gathering is well attended by both congregation and instrumentalists, and a stepped platform, always a hallmark of

these gatherings seemingly, has been put against the north wall of the farm near its meeting with School Lane. This has enabled the younger members of the gathering to see into the service and lend a voice to the singing just as well as any of the much taller adults.

This picture shows the instrumentalists, who often led the chapel choir, with their double bass, cello and fiddlers on the various engagements of the Methodist calender through the year. The occasion we are looking at here is the seasonal stout-hearted trek to the outlying farmsteads of the village. Carols would be played for the dwellers who otherwise may not have enjoyed much in the way of Christmas cheer, due to geographic isolation. The carols played here were the local ones like 'Good News' and 'Hoyland Anthem'. If the playing went on into the darkness hours, they would read their music by the light of oil lamps. Their stop here was at Kemp Spout. Of the people I have been able to name in this picture; at far right, the last violinist we can see is Alonza Ellison, who actually lived at Kemp Spout, and at the extreme left in a bowler hat is Mr. Charles Slater, the conductor.

In another gathering, this time on Whit Monday at Bitholmes Farm, we can see how Whitsuntide got its name. Traditionally the schoolchildren of a village would be wearing new clothes at this festival of the seventh week after Easter. Here they are recorded as the 'Brightholmlee Scholars'. White clothes would predominate, especially

amongst the girls; hence the word from white ..'Whit'. This was considered to be a great time for christenings too. In this 1905 picture, initialled by Luther Fairest, the worshipers have gathered outside Mr. Grayson's barn, and are carrying the older chapel banner, which preceded the one which most present villagers remember.

Here the Sunday School of Oughtibridge Zion Chapel are having their 'Whit Walk', complete with banner. This street walk, with the Sunday School youngsters in bright new clothes, or such that could be afforded, would finish with an outdoor service and hymns. This picture was taken in 1927, along the stretch of terraced houses on Langsett Road, opposite from the bread shop.

Closest to us is Mr. Hammerton; then, holding the near end of the banner is George Hirst. The man with the bowler hat holding the far end of the banner is Willie Walters. By tradition the chapel followers walked in the morning, and the church ones in the afternoon of Whit Sunday.

This meeting (over), more numerously attended, had the assistance of a public address system and a pianist on the back of a lorry. The year was 1953, and the stop here was the junction of Bridge Hill and Low Road, just outside the Cock Inn; which then had Henry Cousins as the landlord.

Oughtibridge Band is in attendance here. We see them striking up a tune as the banner is just arriving at the site. This part of Oughtibridge, the foot of Bridge Hill, has traditionally been used for public gatherings and meetings since earliest recorded history.

Dwellings (and Landscape)

When we talk about houses which are representative of the richer classes of people within an area, it is generally accepted that different regions will give rise to differing ideas as to how a 'better-off' person's house will appear. In the case of Wharncliffe Side, the idea which normally strikes the onlooker to dwellings of this category is not so much grandeur, as a sort of thoughtful individuality and good integration with the landscape. A list which readily comes to mind is:- Spring Grove House, built in the 1850s, and added to in the latter years of the 19th century by Mr. Joseph Dixon, Dyson Holmes House built in 1794, and Old Hall Farm, which strictly speaking is in the neighbouring hamlet of Brightholmlee, but represents the settlement in its earlier form. There is also the tower house in Glen Howe which we have seen, and Damasel House, of which there is no historical photograph that I have yet been able to find. Scattered amongst these landmarks were the humble dwellings of the blade-makers, filesmiths, tennant farmers, mill workers, quarry workers, drift miners and brick makers which also made up the features of this rural valley.

Spring Grove House stood just alongside, and to the west of the main road through the village, but situated in such a way as to be quite secluded from it. It was basicly a Victorian house which was enlarged in several stages, and given a mock-Tudor, black and white half-timbered facade facing south-east. This continued around that end of the house to form an octagonal solarium facing east. The solarium was topped by a cupola with a weather vane on top of it, in a kind of London Tudor style. The main entrance was to the south, reached by both a woodland drive from the main road, and a gateway on Green Lane. The south entrance was in the form of a porch in an angle of the house, which had an ornamental arrangement of battlements on top of it. This and the heavy wooden door with its iron studs echoed the style of a castle. On the grounds in front of the house was a rockery, and then, lower down, tennis courts.

The domestic staff of Spring Grove in Edwardian times consisted of three women, a chauffeur and a gardener. This was quite a normal complement for a house of that size at the time. This picture was taken near the south entrance, and shows a parlour maid, scullery maid and housekeeper/cook. In the rising grounds behind the house was a walled garden with a greenhouse, typically like that of a Victorian kitchen garden. There was also a scenic footpath called 'Canadian Walk', which started just beyond the garden wall and ran in a southerly direction through very picturesque woodland and cliffside scenery, towards Oughtibridge. The whole thing was set in a wood of its own, Usher Wood. Parts of the wood were liberally planted with rare and unusual trees, brought back from Mr. Dixon's foreign travels. The house itself survived until the 1970s.

DYSON HOLMES   HR.

Here we see the house which was called 'Dyson Holmes', in a picture initialled by Herbert Robinson. Like Spring Grove House, it too stood not far from the main road. It can be found half way down a winding, wooded lane, Dyson Holmes Lane, which starts across the road from the Blue Ball Inn. This was Joseph Dixon's other residence, an older house in fact than Spring Grove, and the one which the Dixons decided to live in when they first came to the valley. Here Joseph lived whilst Spring Grove was being

74

built up to his requirements. Dyson Holmes dates from the 1790s, and looks much the same now in front view, as it did when this 1908 picture was taken. Herbert has again pictured some of the domestic staff of the Dixon households. The woman on the right was pictured in the photograph of the housemaids at Spring Grove, so it is reasonable to assume that she worked at both houses. The chap in the middle is evidently a gardener. Dyson

Holmes never had a very large garden, so it is probable that he had tasks at both houses. The third member of the group is evidently another woman in domestic service, as she is wearing an apron. There appears to be a calm homely atmosphere at the house, which on the whole seems to be widely reflected in the faces of many of the Dixon's employees.

Most of the written and spoken comments that I have come across seem to record Mr. Dixon as being a very good, fair and not un-generous employer, a philanthropist of the valley and of Oughtibridge through most of his time here. Although Joseph and his family came to Dyson Holmes House at the time of the mill's purchase in 1871, his father Peter didn't come until 1879. Once there, old Peter lived on for only three more years, passing away peacefully in the house on 2nd January 1882, at the age of sixty two. The firm continued however to be called Peter Dixon & Son Ltd.

Dumpling Hall was built in the early part of the 19th century, and carries a datestone of 1818 on a low outbuilding just out of sight to the right, on the end wall. Pictured here in 1906, this building has quite a history. It was used as a police station in Victorian times, and had a small lockup included for the detaining of miscreants. There is a fair amount of underground water in this area. The cellar of the building has a well in it, and two water spouts from seperate springs once fed a horse trough, which still lies in the area just off the pavement in the foreground, hidden here by the grass verge. The trough has the date of 1875 carved on it. It was

always said that one of the spouts gushed water pure enough for domestic use; i.e. for drinking water, and many villagers filled their jugs and pails there daily for just that

purpose. The other alas was only good enough to let run into the trough for the horses. As a village dweller it would have been imprinted on you at an early age which was the good spout!

The motifs around the door case are supposed to represent rolling pins and dumplings in a stylised way, and could be another reference to the local fondness for making bilberry dumplings. During alterations done by the present owner an oven was found built into an internal wall of this house. The local W.I. made some historical research around that time, and claim to have found that, as well as housing the coachman for Spring Grove House, it also catered for some of the extra baking requirements of the big house. Here Herbert has taken in a broad sweep of Wharncliffe valley for a picture taken in

the winter of 1908. He was looking down from a field locally called the 'Donkey Field' to Green Lane and School Lane beyond. The school can be seen roughly in the middle of the picture, and behind that are the fields which form the centre of the village today. The far backdrop of the picture shows Wharncliffe Chase on the right, and the hill known as 'Saddleback' on the left, marking the entrance to the neighbouring valley of Ewden. Closer to the camera, in the left foreground is the cluster of buildings known as Damasel Cottages, and on the right is Joseph Dixon's house Spring Grove. Looking at this house from the back shows how rambling it appeared there compared to the smarter side which faced downhill. Mr. Dixon repeatedly added new rooms and extensions for the convenience of himself and his family, till it appeared as here, a huddle of gables, roofs and chimnies. The drive up from the bottom entry gate wound through woodland scenery trimmed with Rhododendrons, and was carefully designed to show off the pleasing side of the building. Visitors, guests and potential business clients would come in this way, so it was important to impress them. Servants and tradesmen had to go in at the back, where a gatehouse regulated comings and goings. Other Victorian industrialists were known to go to similar or even more elaborate lengths with their homes. The gun manufacturer Armstrong organised a twisting woodland approach road so that it revealed facinating views of his grand house 'Cragside', north of Newcastle. These views increase in interest as the lane dips in and out of the woods for the last few hundred yards. The idea was to impress, in a stage-managed way.

Moving in closer shows us several new details rarely seen in photographs of this time. Brook Lane starts near the bottom left and travels up diagonally, passing what is now known as the 'Plantation' on its right, to become School Lane. School Lane then passes the old school and joins on to the main road at the right of the picture. The main road can then be seen curving out of the valley towards Stocksbridge. The Blue Ball Inn and the chapel can

just be seen at the point where the road disappears from view. Amongst the sparsely spread houses that are visible in this scene, the one streaked with ivy near the centre of the picture was known as Mr. Robinson's. It was, in fact divided into three cottages and he lived in the farthest one.

This is the row of cottages which was called 'Kemp Spout', pictured on April 23rd 1908. Some late snows still clung to the hills in that year. This is the place where the group of chapel instrumentalists stood for the picture shown earlier. We are at a 'T'

junction at the top of Green Lane. The left turn continues the upward journey to 'Hilltop', and the right turn runs level for a short distance before descending as Storth Lane towards Glen Howe. The outbuildings visible to the left housed a filesmith's workshop, run by Alonza Ellison. Out of these four dwellings, three carried ground floor shutters; the age-old means of sealing the house from the elements at night. These houses survived until around 1971.

Coming down Green Lane a short distance from Kemp Spout, we get to Damasel Cottages, seen here with a group of villagers outside looking dressed as if about to set off for Sunday worship. Bowler hats, Derby hats, waistcoats and starched collars are the order of the day here. Watch chains would be seen spanning from one waistcoat pocket to the other, passing through a button hole on the way, as part of a 'Sunday Best' outfit. A track called Damasel Lane led off from Green Lane at this point, but it is no longer in use at this end.

This picture shows the full layout of Damasel Cottages as they stood in 1905, with four dwellings in evidence. These simple but sturdy houses, on the hillside before Howe Wood were typical of the many cottages which came into the posession of the Dixons when they acquired the nearby paper mill in 1871. Joseph's policy of low rents, coupled with what were considered decent factory wages in late Victorian times, persuaded many of his workers to stay local and loyal through several generations. Looking back from Brook Lane towards Green Lane produced this view back in 1910. Spring Grove House can be seen again almost tucked away in the woods to the left.

Further down still and we see the lower part of Green Lane. Two horses in tandem are pulling a cart up the hill. They seem to know the way by themselves; no driver sits with them, and no-one needs to lead them. It could have been that the man walking closest to them was the owner, and that this journey was familiar to them, to the extent that they needed no prompting. To the left we can see the house known as 'Glen Ville', which at this time was home to a family called Senior. This building has recently been demolished, and its grounds developed into a close huddle of residential housing. The rising land behind belonged, in the upper part to Swinnock Hall Farm, and was in fairly continuous use as dairy pasture. The brook enters this scene from the left, behind Glen Ville, and travels towards the Don off beyond the right hand side of the picture. A footbridge crosses the water on Brook lane at the bottom right.

The large semi-detached house in the centre nowadays has three dwellings in it. Not long after this picture was taken several more houses were built on the roadside to the left. Damasel Cottages are visible again in this picture, up past the double bend in Green Lane, and again on the skyline we can see Hill End House.

Up at the northern end of the village stood Blue Ball cottages (previous page), a group of dwellings beside the road between the Blue Ball Inn and the chapel. This was said to have been the residence of Walter Holmes. Three dwellings were originally recorded here, though by the time this picture was taken in 1906 we can see, by the blocked up door, that a merger of two cottages has taken place. These cottages were still here in the 1960s. After they were demolished a development called Brightholmlee Court took their place.

Standing close to Wharncliffe Side, and sometimes mistaken by outsiders as an uphill part of the village is Brightholmlee, a small cluster of grey and mellowed stone buildings on high ground to the west. The name translates from the Saxon as 'Bright Water-Meadow'; and, standing over an old river plain like Ewden, it is easy to see why.

Documents dated 1337 record the activities of a 'John of Brightholmlee', but others are said to point to a date as early as 1200 for the settlement. A pack horse trail called Townfield Lane goes through the middle part of the hamlet. It is generally recognised that the buildings on the uphill side of the track are several hundred years older than the ones below it. The track has carried the knickname 'Lover's Lane' for as far back as living memory can go; due to the good privacy it gives. When walking along it you effectively descend into a cutting made by the wear of cartwheels.

At the upper part of the settlement is High Lea Farm (previous page); a long, single storeyed cruck building with a gabled attic; a type which is now rare. There were several dwellings in this building, three at the time this picture was taken, circa 1905, and latterly two. Now just one dwelling takes up the whole of the inside. During my school years Mr. Marsden was the farmer who lived there, and the other dwelling was occupied by his tennant, Mrs Bullock. Mr. Marsden once told me of a building which had adjoined his outer wall centuries before, on the gable-end to the right. Being an unusual arched construction, it had left traces of that shape in the stonework at that end. In its time this had been a communal bake-house oven, and had been provided by the local lord in the days when Brightholmlee was a manorial posession. Villagers would go there to make their bread and oatcakes daily. It was the heat from the continued baking which, over the years had left the visible trace, which I remember as a slight etching of the stone, with a modest but noticeable change in colour. This mark was the only outward evidence of the hamlet's standing as one-time manorial estate property. Unfortunately within the last twenty years it was obliterated by the insertion of a window in the exact spot. Oughtibridge continued to have a 'parish' communal bake-house till well into the 20th century.

Brightholmlee 'Old Hall Farm' is just a few yards down the road from High Lea, but slightly set back from the road, and in a yard of its own between two barns. Here is a house which is thought to be Tudor, or perhaps earlier in origin. When entering at the front door in the middle of the picture and looking to the right you see probably the oldest fireplace in the area, in unchanged condition. This was commented on by the Stocksbridge historian Joseph Kenworthy; in his histories of the region written between the two world wars. The way it and its chimney joined into the frame of the

house, he said, is a pointer to the antiquity of the hall. This is another 'Cruck' dwelling, having two pairs of crucks in its skeleton; and there seems to have originally been three. Old Hall Farm has been the property of the Appleyard family since the 18th century, when they first came to the hamlet as farmers and owners of land with valuable lead seams. The house is still occupied by a nephew of the Appleyard family, Mr. Tom Shaw. The additions we can see on either side of the hall are actually part of it, but date from different times. The left hand addition dates from around 1620, and to the right is a building from around 1711.

A few steps down from the Old Hall Farm; and we are at the turnoff of Townfield Lane, the old packhorse track which once led to Bolsterstone. These cottages, which stood at the start of the lane were used as farmworkers dwellings for most of their existance, and were indeed still in use as such until the early 1970s. Unfortunately they were demolished shortly after the hamlet was designated as a conservation area around the middle of that decade. Structural problems were cited as the reason for this; though it seems like a poor apology for the loss of a vernacular building within a protected hamlet. The building which stands there now has tried to reproduce the feel and style of a cottage, and carries the name 'Stone Troughs'.

Then and Now

The Wharncliffe Arms has retained much of its outside appearance between the years of 1907 and the late 1990s when the modern picture (opposite) was taken. When Walter Holmes and his four-legged friend stood in front of it, it catered for a small, close-knit rural community, and for the passing traffic of a horse-drawn age. Stables like the one on the right were in fairly regular use.

A survey and valuation of public houses of the area, carried out by William Stead of Owlerton in 1857 recorded that there was in those earlier days a club room over this stable. The room was equipped, it said, with various games; Bagatelle, "French Bagatelle", Quoits, Dominoes and, for the musically minded, "two Fiddles".

Because the Wharncliffe Arms was not owned by a brewery then, the building had its own brewing equipment; and the list went on to mention two brewing tubs in an outside brewhouse, forty one 18-gallon barrels, a "work flaskit" and several other brewing implements. This entry to the survey was concluded by the statement:"Included in the premises were two filecutting shops where some 14 men could work and no doubt act as custom to the house."

It is still possible to see some of the stone "stocks" on which files were made, mounts for the 'stiddies', in the area at the back of the pub.

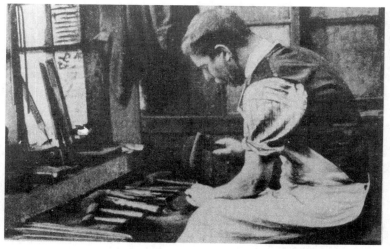

A typical filesmith at work at his 'Stiddy' anvil.

85

The area at the bottom of Bridge Hill has changed from being the relaxed meeting place of Whitsuntide worship in the 1950s to the busy junction on Low Road that we now know. Festooned with traffic signs, and now part of a one-way system, it would be difficult for such a size of congregation to gather here at the present day. The houses which were across the way from the pub have made way for a hedge, now bordering someone's garden. This modern-day picture was taken in April 2004.

The Travellers Inn has had a chequered history in the time between the 1908 picture and this picture of the late 1990s. After losing its licence sometime in the early 1930s, a succession of owners ran a general grocery store there; the Crawshaws, Mr. Percy Badger, Mr. Wordsworth and latterly Mr. & Mrs Clethero. At some period in its life it was known as a 'beerhouse', ie a public house which didn't sell wines and spirits, only ale. Such a pub is now quite a rarity, and the last known one to exist in Sheffield was the Great Britain in John Street.

Almost at the highest point of Brightholmlee is High Lea Farm, a good place to compare Luther Fairest's 1905 picture with a modern one. High Lea nowadays stands near the boundary line where the Peak District National Park begins, and this photo, taken on a May 3rd 2004 shows how comparatively little time has changed the old farmstead building.

Part of Old Hall Farm still looks out on Townfield Lane, reminding walkers that the 18th century Appleyard family were amongst the wealthier of the farming landowners hereabouts. Both they and the nearby Grayson family owned land with valuable lead deposits, used extensively for glass and pottery manufacture, as well as in house construction. The historian Kenworthy records that this building suffered slightly by fire, and was reduced in length from its 1711 dimensions when eventually repaired. In its present form it has no external door, and can only be entered from Old Hall itself. This building is a joy to walk past now just as much as when the top picture was taken circa 1920.